CONCENTRATION

AN APPROACH TO MEDITATION

CONCENTRATION

AN APPROACH TO MEDITATION

BY

ERNEST WOOD

A QUEST BOOK

Published under a grant from The Kern Foundation

THE THEOSOPHICAL PUBLISHING HOUSE
Wheaton, Ill., U.S.A.
Madras, India / London, England

Copyright 1949

The Theosophical Publishing House, India

Revised edition 1949 The Theosophical Publishing House,
Adyar, India.

14th Indian edition 1966.

Quest Book edition 1967 published by The Theosophical Publishing House, Wheaton, Ill., a department of The Theosophical Society in America, by arrangement with The Theosophical Publishing House, Adyar, India.

Second Quest Book printing 1968.

Third Quest Book printing 1970.

Fourth Quest Book printing 1972.

ISBN: 0-8356-0176-5.

Library of Congress Catalog Card Number 67-2874.

Manufactured in the United States of America.

FOREWORD

MR. ERNEST WOOD is well known as both a writer and a lecturer on religious and educational matters, and his work is always careful and thoughtful. A practical course on Concentration is a subject for which he is well equipped, and this little work should prove very useful to the serious student. It is admirably planned, and effectively carried out, and—a most important fact in such a treatise—there is nothing in it which, when practised, can do the striver after concentration the least physical, mental or moral harm. I can therefore heartily recommend it to all who desire to obtain control of the mind.

ANNIE BESANT

AUTHOR'S PREFACE

THIS book has been through a great many editions in various languages—so many that I have long lost track of them—and must have had a total circulation of over a quarter of a million in many countries. In view of public demand for the work I have revised it for this ninth Indian edition, which I hope will be copied in other countries. I have seen no reason to alter materially either the exercises or the philosophy it contains, but I have I think described and explained them better than before.

The book is intended as a practical manual, and the student who takes it seriously as such will derive most benefit from it if he treats it as a six months' course rather than as a reading book. At the end of the course the earnest student will find that he knows exactly what to do next. All the same, others who wish to treat it only as a general help to their meditations will find benefit from reading it through, and picking out for their use whatever appeals especially to themselves.

Many hard-headed people may think that my convictions as to the possibilities which we may attain in the near or remote future by internal self-culture are excessively extravagant; but I can assure them that they are perfectly in accordance with the practical mysticism of both East and West, and are consistent with the actual experience and attainment of a number of experts whom I have had the honour to meet and know.

E. W.

1949

CONTENTS

CHAPTER I

SUCCESS IN LIFE

THE UNLIMITED OPPORTUNITY

Do you desire success in life? Will you take the means that infallibly secure it? Will you choose, and say to yourself: "I will have wealth; I will have fame; I will have virtue; I will have power"? Let your imagination play upon the thought, and watch the dim clouds of hope shape themselves into heavenly possibilities. Give wings to your fancy, for fairer than any picture that you can paint with thought is the future that you can claim with will. Once you have imagined, once you have chosen, say: "I will." And there is nothing on earth that can hinder you for long; for you are immortal and the future is obedient to you.

You say that death may stand in your way? It will not. You say that poverty and sickness and friends may stand in your way? They certainly will not. Nothing can, unless you permit it, or even make it so. But you must choose, and never again must you wish for anything. But you must say: "I will." And you must say it always in thought and in deed, not only now in word. And henceforth never for a moment must your purpose change, but your constant intention must turn everything you touch into line with it. Then, if that which you have chosen is not harmful, it will be yours before long.

You speak of the littleness of man, lost in the wrinkles of giant mother earth, herself as a speck of dust in the infinitudes of space! It is not so, for the great things are not measured by size. You talk of weakness and fatigue, of the immediate follies and pleasures and proprieties and accidents of life—how these confine and limit little man. It is not so, for all can be turned to use. The body is only a garment and the senses but peep-holes in the veil of flesh, and when these are quiet and that is obedient, and the mind dwells in contemplation of your immortal possibilities, a window opens within you, and through it you see and know that you shall be what you will to be, and nothing else.

As the tiny seed, buried in the ground, bursts and puts forth a tender shoot, which pushes its way through the soil and wins its freedom in the upper air, and presently there is a mighty oak, peopling the earth with portions of itself, or, as a great banyan spreads without limit from a little root, providing wealth and home for myriads of creatures; so put ye forth this day the first tender but not uncertain shoot of will, and choose what you will be.

What will you choose? Will you have power? Then let others be freer and more powerful because you are so. Will you have knowledge? Then let others be wiser because you are so. Will you have love? Then let others enjoy it because you have much to give. Thus will your will be in accord with that first and universal principle of being which becomes increasingly known to each of us, and instils in time the prime lesson of that unshrinking sympathy which will ultimately make all strength our strength and all life our life.

What will be your means? Everything that you meet, small and great; for there is nothing that you cannot use as a means to your end.   But once more, let all the persons and the things that you use be benefited by the use.   Thus your success will be theirs also, and the first principle will be fulfilled.

SUCCESS AND CONCENTRATION

But, whatever you choose, one thing you will need in all things and at all times—concentration of purpose, of thought, of feeling, of action; so that this, like a powerful magnet, will polarize everything with which you deal.   In all the aims of life it is needed for success.   The men who have succeeded in business, social and political life, in art, science and philosophy, in power and virtue, have all been marked out by a constancy of purpose and an easy control of mind. Has it not happened always, is it not happening now, and will it not happen in the future, that so far as human progress is in human hands it is achieved by systematic and persistent activity, control of desires and concentration of mind, and without these it is not achieved?

Read the lives and philosophy of every type of purposeful men, and you will find this fact recorded in them.   The Epicurean of old concentrated his mind upon the present and tried to live in accord with natural laws.   He did not allow his mind to dwell with regret upon anything past, nor to have fears or anxieties for the future.   The Stoic fixed his attention upon the things which lay in his control, refusing to be disturbed by anything that lay outside his power and purpose, or to waste thought and feeling upon it. The Platonist strove to fix his mind, with reverent inquiry, upon the mysteries of life. Patanjali, the great master of Indian Yoga, declared that man could come to his own true state only by the successful practice of complete control of mind. The religious devotee strives, by filling his life and surroundings with ceremonies and symbols, and by constantly repeating in thought the names of God, to stimulate his mind to ever stronger and stronger devotional feelings. The successful man of knowledge is so intent upon his purpose that he finds instruction in the most trifling things that he meets. Such is the power of mind that with its aid all things can be bent to our purpose, and such is the power of man that he can bend the mind to his will.

Do we not find that indecision, trepidation, anxiety and worry give rise to bodily ills, weakness, indigestion and sleeplessness? Even in these small matters regular practice of control of mind, in a simple form, acts like a magic cure. It is the best means of escape from envy, jealousy, resentment, discontent, delusion, self-deception, pride, anger and fear. Without it, the building of character cannot be carried on, and with it it cannot fail. Any study is successful in proportion to the mental concentration brought to bear upon it; and the practice largely increases the reproductive powers of memory.

The Higher Achievements

One of the higher efforts and achievements of concentration of mind has been well described by

Dr. Annie Besant in her book *The Ancient Wisdom*, in the following words:

"The student must begin by practising extreme temperance in all things, cultivating an equable and serene state of mind; his life must be clean and his thoughts pure, his body held in strict subjection to the soul, and his mind trained to occupy itself with noble and lofty themes; he must habitually practise compassion, sympathy, helpfulness to others, with indifference to troubles and pleasures affecting himself, and he must cultivate courage, steadfastness and devotion. Having, by persevering practice, learned to control his mind to some extent, so that he is able to keep it fixed on one line of thought for some little time, he must begin its more rigid training by a daily practice of concentration on some difficult or abstract subject, or on some lofty object of devotion. This concentration means the firm fixing of the mind on one single point, without wandering, and without yielding to any distractions caused by external objects, by the activity of the senses, or by that of the mind itself. It must be braced up to an unswerving steadiness and fixity, until gradually it will learn so to withdraw its attention from the outer world and from the body that the senses will remain quiet and still, while the mind is intensely alive with all its energies drawn inwards to be launched at a single point of thought, the highest to which it can attain. When it is able to hold itself thus with comparative ease, it is ready for a further step, and by a strong but calm effort of the will it can throw itself beyond the highest thought it can reach while working in the physical brain, and in that effort will rise to and unite itself with the higher consciousness and find itself free of the body."

The literature of religion is full of instances of remarkably extended vision of unseen things attained by the rapt mind. Indian yogis enumerate eight sets of faculties and powers, including vision of the absent, the past and the future, psychic telephony, telescopy, and microscopy, the power of travelling invisibly in the subtle body, and others—all attainable by concentration.   Marvellous as these effects are and fascinating as are the study and the practice of them to many, they present only one of the developments through concentration.

In another direction, many thinkers look upon these as small matters in comparison with the discovery of the god within us, and declare that we need only to find the place of peace within ourselves to achieve the fulfilment of human life.   They, too, extol concentration as the means.

Thus thousands of people all over the world are now turning to the practice of concentration as a first step towards new developments in human life—of which man himself, not his environment, will be the cause.

Still there are many more thousands who value the practice for its known benefits in the familiar spheres of every-day life.   These are the people who say: "We do not want fascinating novelties; we want ordinary life to be saner than it is—thought clearer, love cleaner, will calmer—and we will leave to destiny any larger future that may be ours."

In every case concentration does not mean a narrowing, limiting or confining of our thoughts and activities, nor any loss of human sympathies and interests.   It

·does not mean retiring to the forest or the cave, with the wine of life run dry in our veins like a desert river in the summer drought. It does mean that the whole of our life becomes polarized to a chosen purpose animated by increased powers of thought, love and will, and inspired with a higher self than we have known before.

CHAPTER II

THE MAGIC BOX

THE MIND'S FIRST POWER

YEARS ago I described the contents and workings of the mind as a magic box, comparing it to the nest of boxes produced by an Oriental conjuror, who spreads his carpet and lays a box in the middle of it, then takes a number of boxes out of that box, and then a number of boxes out of each of those, until the whole carpet is piled up with boxes. I compared these boxes to ideas in the mind and described how one idea contains or gives rise to innumerable others.

Now, in order to describe the nature of the contents and working of the mind, I will pick at random an advertisement in the daily newspaper. It reads as follows: "Artistic luxury home. Hillside. Magnificent trees. 6 bedrooms. 4 bathrooms . . ."

What does this advertisement do to me? It does very much the same as I do when I press the self-starter in my car. It sets the engine going. I can then sit still in the car and let the engine tick over while I decide where to go, or I can connect it with the transmission and steering mechanism and start my journey to a definite place.

In my mind the ticking over begins: "Home"—I instinctively and almost unconsciously say to myself, and at once several memory-pictures spring up. Several! Nay, thousands of them; homes in which I have lived—in my childhood, youth, maturity and elderliness—in which I have visited, which I have looked at as I passed them by on the road, which I have seen pictured in magazines. . . . And if for one fraction of a second I allow myself to dwell upon one of these homes, thousands of details arise. Perhaps it is a door that I look at. Immediately there are hundreds and hundreds of doors of various sizes and colours and patterns—even of several shapes—standing and pushing around and jostling one another, and seeming to call out: "Look at me! Look at me!"

I will not try to compute the number of these memory pictures in my mind, nor what future hordes of them will arise with further experience. But I will acknowledge that every slightest one can proliferate prodigiously. It reminds me of that old story of an Eastern potentate who promised a boon to one of his courtiers, who then asked for one grain of rice for the first square on the chess board, two for the second, four for the third, and so on to the last of the sixty-four squares—a boon which the monarch smilingly granted, little recking that it would bankrupt his whole kingdom, in fact all the kingdoms of the earth, and of many earths.

In my mind I find, too, homes that might have been and homes that may be in the future—re-arrangements and re-combinations of the part of the homes that I have seen. In this manner I can enter the realm of imagination as well as of fact, and I may even think of birds' homes and worms' homes and gnomes' homes and heavenly homes—there is almost no end to this.

But there comes an end to the process, for something inside me says: "Among all these, which do you want to possess or to contemplate?" Now arise two further powers of the mind. I find myself saying: "I like this. I do not like that," and thereupon pushing some of the memory-pictures away out of sight and inviting others to stay. This is the love-process.

Then comes a decision: "This one I want. To this I will go. I will work for this. I will contemplate this." Now the mere ticking-over ceases, the transmission is engaged and the steering begins.

DISCOVERY OF THE WILL

In the previous section I have described a mind-cycle, beginning with a coruscation or up-welling of ideas of mental pictures, continued with a desire and ending with a decision to act. We started the engine ticking over, engaged the transmission and then handled the steering wheel. This process is a full cycle, for at this point the ideas begin to flow again, but in a prescribed direction determined by the will.

Sit down quietly and comfortably, and very slowly and gently bring your attention to a particular thing and watch what happens. I will give an example. While I write this I am lying—as it happens—on my back on the grassy slopes of a Hollywood hillside garden, holding a stiff little book aloft in my left hand, and a pencil in my right. My left wrist gets tired, so I have to lower the book now and then, which is beneficial, being conducive to frequent reflective thought. On my right is a lemon tree, which gives me pleasant dappled shade from the rays of the slanting afternoon sun. On my left are two large bushes and an orange tree, backed by over-towering pines. In front at a distance I see portions of a handsome house and, in the near foreground, a fine palm tree, some thirty feet tall. Let me shut my eyes and think only of the palm.

A procession of mind-pictures begins. Here comes a palm grove in South India in a garden where I lived for many years. In the midst of that palm grove was a pond; I find myself now in thought standing on the edge of it and looking at the water-lilies there—blue lotuses. And then (of all unexpected things—I have not directed my thoughts) a blue crayon and myself sitting at a desk at school fifty-five years ago. I still watch disinterestedly, and now comes some map drawing at school—a map of India with coloured coast lines. Now a part of the map—I am writing the word Hyderabad near the north-west corner (a true memory), and now the river Indus is drawn in. My thought jumps again twenty-five years: I become Principal of the College at Hyderabad—talking to the students at Assembly—a lecture in Physics— a glass tube—glass—Venetian glass—a curio shop— an old rocking chair—a cradle—a baby—and so on.

Such is the mental process when the driver is not there. The car goes along a road, but not of my conscious present choice. I notice incidentally that *I* do not produce the welling-up of the images, and *I* do not even produce the drifting flow of thoughts but I *am* the director, if and when I direct them. At other times I am merely the looker-on, just as I may be the looker-on at my own blood-stream or digestive process.

Now stop thinking about me. Select your own "palm tree"—any object. Look at it, then close your eyes, and watch for yourself within your own mind the drift of mental pictures and ideas. Do this several times with different objects, then observe that you can stop the drift by stepping into the stream and directing it. To do this you have to pounce upon one of the objects in the drift. You hold it and see what you can do with it. You watch its up-wellings or coruscations and you next deliberately select one of these and watch *its* up-wellings, and thus go on directing the flow of thought.

As an illustration of this process, let me suppose that your "palm tree" of the moment is a cow. That is what has caught your mental eye, and now you hold it and watch its up-welling. Here, standing around it, together with it, are the ideas milk, calf, horns, bull, shed, field, grass, your Uncle's favourite black cow, patience, gentleness, and many, many others. Among these you deliberately select, let us say, grass, and now you allow grass to up-well, and again deliberately select. It is the power of selection that is now to be observed and learnt; we will make use of the other processes further on.

From this mental experiment you will get a new sense of power, which is the power of concentration, operated by the will. You will also get a new knowledge and experience of "I". A third gain is that you will have learned how to think, as I will explain more fully later on.

THE ROADS OF THOUGHT

The drift which I have so carefully described and you, I hope, have inspected in your own mind, is not a bad thing nor a disorderly one. It is the relaxed condition of the mind, and we can use it for resting when we are mentally tired. In the course of prolonged study involving mental effort we may stop awhile to rest and recuperate by simply leaning back, closing the eyes, relaxing the body—especially the neck—and quietly watching the mental drift.[1] It is not healthy to be thinking all the time. Thinking is intended for acquiring knowledge or applying knowledge. It is not essential living.

That the drift is not something disorderly and without cause and system I will now show, by describing what I have called the Four Roads of Thought.[2]

These are sometimes called the associations of ideas, but, strictly speaking, that term would refer to the effects of Contiguity only, i.e., to remembered things, their parts and qualities and familiar contacts, and remembered thoughts about them.

It will be a case of Contiguity if, when I go out in my car this evening, I have a collision with another car at the corner of Hollywood Boulevard and Vine Street. We will assume that this is enough to give me a nervous shock or even some injury, but not enough to put me out of action. I have been in two such accidents—one in Wales and one in India—in which the cars were terribly

[1] I want to warn some readers against the habit of mental relaxation into ideas of sensuous experience, which is not uncommon. Some people do this to induce sleep. Looking at the mental drift, if continued, will induce sleep also, and it is a much better way. It induces sleep with full mental relaxation and does not conduce to dreams.

[2] For the full exposition of the Four Roads of Thought, including the sub-divisions of them, making nine in all, see *Mind and Memory Training* by Ernest Wood, published by Sir Isaac Pitman and Sons, Ltd., London, England. However, that full exposition is not required for the practice of Concentration, though necessary in memory training.

damaged but I came out almost unhurt. These two accidents remain vividly in memory, so that any mention of the places Holywell and Devala, where they occurred, will instantaneously bring them, with many attendant details, into my mental view. At present, mention of the intersection of Hollywood and Vine does not bring up thoughts of a sickening blow and crumpled cars, but rather pictures of a large Bank building and streams of pedestrians crossing at the signal of a green light and a semaphore marked "go". But if I have a similar accident at that place I shall thenceforth have a strong association of that place and the event, so that my pedestrians and my Bank will sink to the status of second and third quality associations in connection with the thought of that intersection of streets.

The strength of associations of ideas is due to (1) vivid or emphatic experience of two things in conjunction, as related above, or (2) frequent repetition in conjunction of two things which are not vivid or emphatic in experience. An example of the latter cause of association is the learning that in French "livre" means "book," which the student usually achieves by repeating " livre," and "book" close together a number of times.

This forming of associations goes on not only in connection with our own experience, but also with what we have read or been told.

Before closing this piece of description of Contiguity, I must mention that we have juxtapositions in time as well as in space, in the form of familiar sequences. Thus a darkly lowering cloud leads to the expectation of rain, or in American towns, a peculiar tinkling nursery tune sounding in the street presages the arrival of an ice-cream van. In this manner also the letter A recalls B rather than, say, Q or X. Such are the time Contiguities, sometimes amounting to the invariable sequence dubbed cause and effect in the material sciences.

The other Three Roads of Thought are: (2) Class Relationship, or logical inclusion; (3) Whole and Part, or concrete inclusion; and (4) Object and Quality or functional inclusion.

Suppose I am instructing a group. Several people are sitting before me and I utter the word "cow". One person may think of a brown cow, another of a black one; myself, I am thinking of a five-legged cow which an old friend of mine saw in India and wrote about. Someone may jump from the class-concept "cow" to the bigger class-concept "animal". Thus we see together an object and its class, and the mind passes easily along that road from one to the other. If I suddenly say "pencil" and ask you for the first word that comes up you may give me the Contiguity "hand" or "paper," or, following this second Road of Thought, you may call out "typewriter," having gone through its class to another member of the same class of things. If I pronounce "chair," you might say "my mother's rocking chair," or possibly "furniture," or, if your Road of the moment is Contiguity, you might call out "cushion," thinking of an experience of a cushion on a chair.

There are still two other Roads of Thought which you may follow in these cases. One is that of Analysis or concrete inclusion. This gives the relation between whole and part of an object. It may lead from "cow" to "horns," horns being part of a cow, or from "chair" to "back" or "legs".

Fourthly, we have the Road of Quality or functional inclusion, from which may arise innumerable adjectives, such as "old" or "new" "soft" or "hard," "figured" or "plain," "big" or "little," "round" or "square," "blue" or "green," "quick" or "slow". For example, "tortoise" may give rise to "slowness", "elephant" may give rise to "strength". To a Hindu mind, which often tends to run on abstract more than concrete lines, "cow" generally calls up "beneficence" or "bounty," for to most of them it has stood since childhood as the chief symbol of that quality. For convenience I give a chart showing examples of the four Roads of Thought.

THE FOUR ROADS OF THOUGHT

Examples:

1. Milk—baby; pen—hand; ship—sea; spade —garden; fatigue—sleep; gluttony—indigestion.

2. Animal—dog; view—landscape; chair—table; red—blue; heat—cold.

3. Car—wheel; tree—root; house—door; root—branch; arm—leg.

4. Earth—round; coin—silver; ice—cold; ink—fluid; lemon—yellow.

Some readers may say that all this sounds rather theoretical and technical. Let me assure them that I have not mentioned these Roads except for the purpose of using them in concentration exercises. Even so, it is quite possible to put the matter in a more general and for some an easier way by saying that there is always a reason for the association of ideas—that if one mental picture gives rise to hundreds of others there will be a precise reason for every one of them, and no mere chance at all in the process.

Thus, if some one asks why he thinks of milk when he hears the word cat, the reason is that this conjunction is a matter of familiar experience. If he thinks of claws, or whiskers, that is because claws and whiskers are part of the cat.

Knowledge of the Roads is valuable for working in a very precise way and getting all you can out of "cat"

THE PRACTICE OF RECALL

We may now turn to the first exercise:

Exercise 1. Study the following diagram:

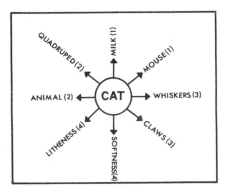

Copy it on a large sheet of paper and try to increase the number of arrows to 100. Write in a Road-nomination or reason for each arrow-word, in the manner shown in number-brackets on the diagram. If you cannot put in 100 at one sitting, keep the diagram and continue the work each day. If you dislike cats, use "dog" or anything else, for it is a rule of mental health not to ponder on disliked things. Do this exercise every day for a week, at least.

Take care not to *think about* the milk, or mouse, or whiskers, etc. Merely notice them and write them down, and then slide your attention back along the arrow to the cat. Do not jump back, but slide back. Then ask yourself, "What next?" while looking at the cat. Again write down any idea that comes up. When you have written down a good many, you may find the mind going empty, and bringing out no more. Still hold on for a while, and only after a little while more begin to use the Four Roads systematically to find some more.

When at last you do decide to give up waiting or looking for more arrow-words, you may stop and think about what you have been doing. You have been doing concentration, practising *return*, and getting to know what it feels like. Incidentally, you have also been tidying up some of the contents of your mind.

Exercise 2. Now decide to concentrate mentally on a cat (or other object) for five minutes. Look at the clock and make a note of the time. Tell yourself that you are going to keep the cat idea in mental focus for five minutes. Don't think about the time, but make a note of it. After a while you will suddenly realize that you are thinking of something else—note the time—and have forgotten the cat in the meantime. Try to find the cause of this. Was it due to a drift beginning with milk, mouse, whiskers or any other of the hundred direct associations standing around the cat? Was it due to the intrusion into the mind of bodily discomfort, disturbed breathing, sense receptions through hearing, sight, smell or touch? Was it due to a thought of failure in your experiment, or to wondering-if-you-can, or anxiety about something, hurt pride, anger, fear, discontent, timidity, worry or anything of this kind? Do this exercise every day for at least a week, and observe the increase of the period of concentration.

Exercise 3. Most important. Do this one every day for a month.

Concentrate as before on a cat, or some other pleasing object. Do not try to think only of the cat, but deliberately send your thought out along the arrows one after another *with the instruction* to look there and return to the centre. Say "milk—cat, mouse—cat, whiskers —cat, claws—cat" and all the rest of your arrows, and then more. Bring into vision everything you can think of that has a direct connection with "cat" by all the four Roads of Thought. When you cannot think of any more still try hard to think of other things without letting the cat fade from the focus of your attention. Hold on to the cat while you try to penetrate the void. Say to youself, "Is there anything more on Road 1, on Road 2, on Road 3, on Road 4?"

Explanation. In this exercise you are controlling your thoughts or ideas with your will. Slowly your will establishes a *habit of recall* which operates under a *mood of concentration.* After you have practised this exercise every day for a month you ought to be able to put on this mood—which is a feeling—on the slightest decision of the will, silently saying, "Now, concentration."

I can give a very good simile for this to all who know how to swim. When going for a swim you arrive at the edge of the pool, and say to yourself, "Now, swimming." "Do I?" you will ask, perhaps with a little surprise, "I never noticed it." No, you did not notice it, but you do say to yourself, "Now, swimming," and instantly a change comes over the body—and you can swim. Even if you are the best of swimmers and you fall into water accidentally, you flounder about like a beginner in the art of swimming until you recover yourself and realize, "Why! I am in the water," and then you almost subconsciously say, "Now, swimming."

It is not different even with walking. We get up and say, "Now, walking." Then we walk, and all the muscles concerned do their work. Psychiatrists will confirm my statement that there are many people not walking this earth but lying in bed or going about in wheel-chairs merely because they have a mind-inhibition which prevents them from saying to themselves, "Now, walking."

When I start teaching this method of recall there is nearly always someone who asks: "But is it not sufficient merely to try to concentrate on something and keep on persistently bringing the mind back to that thing whenever it wanders away from it?"

The answer is "No." In all these matters we must do no violence to body or mind. We are not hard and lofty masters whipping a wild animal into sullen obedience. We are philosophers—people who know how to live. We know that happiness of body and mind consists in their functioning in a manner and degree harmonious to their hereditary structure and environment. We aim at the fulfilment of life, from crown to toes, not the unnatural development of one part at the expense of the rest, for the sake of some particular prideful power.

To command the mind is one thing. To teach it as a willing and happy pupil constantly finding new delights of experience in healthy functioning is quite another. And also the natural way of mind-living, in which thought and love and will all function harmoniously as one, relating us with understanding and all-over purpose to events and our fellow-beings and the well-spring of divine purpose that brings order and joy from the within of our lives, is best. Thus our lives will blossom like the rose, whose beauty and fragrance come from its secret depths—which does not battle for power, which cannot be chiselled or hammered into shape, yet fulfils itself in yielding its best to its order of society, its own circle of living beings. Truly can it be said of such a life that it tells us of fulfilment, harmony, happiness and faith, and in its gracious yielding to the order of its being there is a spiritual consummation—"the dew-drop slips into the shining sea" while "the universe grows I".

I have not gone far afield and forgotten our present study. That mind of ours is to be like the rose, which surrenders itself to no violence, nor proposes to do it to another.

Let me take up another simile for this practical job of learning concentration. You are sitting reading and you have your dog lying beside you. The dog becomes restless. You call out, "Fido, come here, lie down." Fido obeys, but very soon, when you are not looking, he is away again. You call him, and the process is repeated again and again. Similarly, bringing the mind back again and again to the object of concentration teaches it to concentrate under the stern eye of the will, but not to unfold its own powers naturally in more harmonious living. It does not produce the *mood of concentration* and the *habit of recall* which functions within that mood. There is all the difference in the world between the obedience of a slave (called tamasic) and the ordered activity of intelligent co-operation and mental fruitfulness seen in an ideal family (called sâttvic).

I have prescribed a whole month for this exercise. By that time the average reader of this book should be able to give his attention to one thing in tranquil concentration for any reasonable length of time. This will then lead to a great many other things.

CHAPTER III

AIDS TO CONCENTRATION

ATTENTION WITHOUT TENSION

BEFORE you sit down to commence the practice of recall quietly but definitely decide what is to be your object of concentration and for how long you propose to sustain it. Sometimes people sit down and then begin to decide what to do; they start on one object and then change to another because they find it unsatisfactory, and at last they wake up to realize that their time has gone and they have done nothing. It is better to determine before you sit down exactly what you will do, and then say to yourself quite definitely: "I am going to turn my mind to such and such a thing for a quarter of an hour, and I have no concern with anything else in the world during that time." Picture yourself as doing it before you begin. It does not matter what object you select, though it is best to avoid anything large or complex at first. Real objects may be thought of, or pictures, or symbols, and the object should be often changed.

There are great advantages in settling down very quietly into your period of practice, and launching yourself gently into concentration or thought, as you would float a little paper boat upon a pond, for it prevents the adoption of any tension of body or mind.

It is advisable to cultivate a definite posture for your formal meditations, although you may also practise them at odd times in any position in which you may find yourself—for example, in train or bus, in the garden or on the beach, on a couch or in bed.[1] The advantage of having a regular way of sitting is that you develop the neccessary muscles for it by practice and habit, so that you can sit for a long time without bodily tiredness. The object is not to relax the body completely but to acquire a degree of development of the muscles used in a particular mode of sitting such that you can remain for a long time in that position without tiring—just as a soldier learns to stand at attention for a long time on certain parades. At first the body will ache—but that does not matter; choose your posture and adhere to it, and the aches will pass away.

It is not for me to prescribe a particular mode of sitting, but only to say that it should be healthful. In general, I would say: "Do not let the spine be twisted and do not support the back above the waist; put the arms in a restful position, minimizing their weight on the shoulders; let the legs be restful also, and let the whole position be so well balanced that it will require the minimum amount of muscular energy for its retention. And let the neck be stretched and loosened up and then settled into a balanced line."

Sit down quietly, not abruptly, so that the heart action will not be disturbed, quietly poise the body, see that

---

[1] It is impossible to overestimate the value of odd moments. I knew a man who learnt shorthand in such bits of time—little by little—and benefited much by it. Thus, while waiting for buses and trains people can learn languages, with a little book in hand, if only at the rate of one or two new words a day.

the breath is calmly regular, withdraw your attention from objects of smell, taste, sight, touch and sound, and give your attention to the chosen object.

It is quite common for people to set up bodily tenseness when they start to concentrate, on account of the habit in daily life of using the mind only in relation to material things. I think of picking up a heavy weight and at once my breathing changes and my muscular tension adapts itself to the task. On account of this habit you will often see people frowning, clenching their teeth and doubling up their fists when they begin to concentrate. Indeed, in some cases they do not feel that they are really concentrating unless they have such a tenseness. But I warn them that if they concentrate in such a fashion they will bring on headaches or neckaches, and may even carry themselves to the point of a nervous breakdown. In concentration there should be no special feeling in the body at all.

Let me say a word about the eyes. Practise throwing them out of focus, in preparation for your concentration. Otherwise when you imagine the object as being in its usual position a short distance in front of you, even when closed your eyes may focus themselves and perhaps strain themselves to some extent. When we read in old books that in meditation the eyes should be fixed on the tip of the nose we should reflect that this meant, originally, straight in front or in the direction in which the nose is pointing, which means that the eyes would be parallel and out of focus.[1]

[1] e.g. in the *Bhagavad-Gita*, vi, 13, *nasikagra*, often translated as "tip of the nose," may well mean straight in front. Shri Shankaracharya, in his commentary on this verse, says we must read the

I will give a special exercise in unfocusing the eyes, which you can practise at any odd times, to get away from any danger of eye-strain in the course of your practice of concentration.

Stand or sit in front of a vertical mirror, about one foot away from it. Look at a spot between your own eyebrows. Your eyes will be focused to that spot. Now try to look into each eye with each eye, first separately and then both together so that they are parallel, holding a sheet of cardboard vertically between them, if necessary, in the beginning. Notice also that when you think of something such as a distant scene or an abstract idea in memory, your eyes also take on this condition. Practise this until, before you begin to concentrate upon an object, you can feel that you are not focusing your eyes.

Another way to unfocus the eyes is to hold the two index fingers in a straight horizontal line, exactly level with the eyes, about 15 or 18 inches in front, and with the tips touching. Look at the point where they meet, and then look right through that point at a wall or other object at least 15 or 20 feet away. You will now see another finger—floating, as it were—between the two index fingers. Look further into the distance until this floating finger seems to be $2\frac{1}{2}$ to 3 inches long. Your eyes are now unfocussed. Shut them while you are thus looking.

---

expression with the implication "as it were," and adds that actual fixing of the gaze on the tip of the nose would prevent the mind from carrying out the instruction in vi, 25 (for which vi, 13 is a preparation) to concentrate on the Self (*Atmasanstham manah krirtwa*) In v, 27 the instruction is to have the sight between the two eye-brows, meaning exactly the same thing.

For the sake of avoiding eye-strain and also for the sake of success in your concentration, you must not imagine that you are making an effort to look closely at an object in front of your eyes, and you must not have the least idea that you are *holding* the object in front of you mentally or by will power. Realize that the object itself does not wander away, but that it is your attention that tends to wander, so you must merely look at the object just as calmly as you would look at your watch to tell the time, just as lightly as you would hold a feather in your hand.

The development of attention on any object follows a triple course:

(1) "I am not interested." In this there is a sort of sluggishness. We are not interested in things as such. The elementary man and the animal take very little notice of things unless they have been acted upon by them in some way producing pleasure and pain. Their minds have to be stung into action from without, or to satisfy the pangs of a physical hunger that rises inside the body.

(2) "I am interested because I like it," or "I am interested because I dislike it." In the former case there is a memory of pleasure along with the past experience of the object; in the latter, a memory of pain. So now we want to attend to the object to see how we can more fully enjoy it if it pleases us or how we can get rid of it or master it if it gives us displeasure or pain. This kind of attention does not give a true understanding of the object, because we are biased in our view of it.

(3) "I am interested, because I want to understand the nature, qualities and functions of this object." We view it now without the bias of pleasure and pain, setting

those aside to attain correct understanding. Thus in concentration we have to put aside our likes and dislikes, and especially so in meditation, because we want the truth, which can only be seen in a calm appraisal beyond the turbulence of liking and disliking.

So in our practice of concentration we have not only to be sensible with regard to the body, and see that it is (1) not sluggish, and (2) not excited, but (3) calmly functioning. We have also to see with regard to the mind that it is (1) not sluggish, and (2) not excited, but (3) calm. It is only when there is a full activity in the mind in its perfect calmness that we can properly concentrate or meditate on any object, or we can properly think and understand anything at all. So let there be attention without tension in both body and mind.

Natural Images

A story is told about the Greek philosopher Plato and Diogenes the Cynic. One day Diogenes visited Plato. When he came into the room he saw the table covered with a rich cloth, shelves glittering with silver cups and other vessels, and other sumptuous furniture. He took hold of the cloth with force, dragged it onto the floor, and stamped upon it with his feet, saying, "I tread upon Plato's pride." Plato quietly answered: "And with greater pride!"

Of such stories our lives are made up—stories about ourselves and others, some true to fact and others fanciful. True or fanciful, it is the richness of the stories that makes the richness of our lives and it is the richness of our mental power that makes the richness of the stories.

Fact and environment give opportunity, but living has strength, colour and richness only on account of what it brings to opportunity. Therefore better than to seek opportunity is to be prepared for it.

It is richness that I am emphasizing now. Our life depends on richness of mind. The natural is the rich, and can always teach us. I can ask myself now whether I have truly tasted the richness of a yellow envelope—a common thing—which lies upon my table and catches my eye as I write these words. I look at the envelope because of this question. I close my eyes and think of the colour of that thing. I open them again and see the richness of that yellow colour better than before. It feeds my mind; I feel a new delight and enhancement of life—the immediate result of this small but fruitful act, and I acknowledge with thanks the beloved companionship of that common yellow thing.

This is to preface a piece of advice regarding the practice of concentration. Let your mental images be rich and strong, and you will be happy, whatever they are. To be rich and strong they must be natural.

First, in their setting and position. I will imagine a silver cup standing on Plato's table. I come into the room, like Diogenes, but in a better mood. I rest myself on one of Plato's seats. I say to myself, "The silver cup." It is standing on the table—that is the first point of naturalness. It is not floating in the air. Although I shall very soon forget the table in my more absorbed attention to the cup, it is present at the back of my consciousness and makes its unseen contribution to my present experience, which would be far poorer without it. Second, as to its size, shape and colour. These are things in the realm of sight.   I do not say I will see the cup.   That is not intimate enough—there is too much I in it.   Rather I will be the seeing of the cup.   That is a mind-reality in nature—the seeing of the cup.   Why should I thin out that seeing by diluting it with another picture—a picture of "I"?   Let me *be* the seeing, and that "I" will also fade like the table, and become seeing itself for the time being.   Try this, and you will discover the joy of it.   Try it with the first thing that catches your eye, and let your seeing have size, form and colour.

Thirdly, bring in the other senses.   You may try this now, with your book.   You have been holding it without feeling it.   But now close your eyes, put your consciousness into your finger-tips and run them over the book, may I say caressingly?   Feel the texture of cloth and paper.   Why, you can feel the ink on the paper. And feel the edgeness of the edges, and the cornerness of the corners, and the flatness of the flat parts.   And it smells—did you know that?   The ink smells, and the paper smells, and the glue and string and cloth.   The book has weight too—did you notice that?   And when you touch it there is some sound—its own sound, not the sound you would get from touching Plato's silver cup.

Plato's silver cup!   Yes, I will be touching to feel it; and smelling and hearing.   It lives for that and calls me as the flower calls to the bee, and fulfils some of its purpose in our moment's union of living.   So natural and so intimate should be your concentration.

I will think now of Diogenes pulling the cloth off the table.   He *moves*.   In concentration the stillness of still things must be a positive stillness, as though eternity itself were embodied in them, and the moving of moving things must be natural, like flags waving in the breeze, or persons dancing on the village green, or Diogenes pulling the cloth. We are not concentrating on pictures of things, but on the things themselves.

If necessary, ask yourself a series of questions about the object of concentration—as to position, size, shape, colour, texture and all the rest.

CONFIDENCE

Confidence is faith in the continuance and increase of your own mental ability. It is not belief. It is knowledge—the knowledge that there is a constancy in the very constitution of things.

Our planet the earth and its brothers and sisters go steadily on their regular path round the sun. It would be disconcerting indeed if one fine morning we woke up to discover that they had thrown off the harness of their regular occupations and were indulging in some fancies by dancing a Highland Fling or a Spanish Fandango— that is, if we could wake up at all in such circumstances, and were not overwhelmed with disaster at the first disturbance of the regularity and harmony which we call natural law. But there will be no such fancifulness— we are sure of that, even though that surety is only faith. Only faith! Why, faith is the very foundation of all our mind-work and conscious being, of all our sanity. We have an ineradicable faith that the world is sane. And we like this. We think with delight of "the ordered music of the marching orbs".

We are part and parcel of this great sanity, and the axes on which we have grown will not fail us any more than the axis of the earth.   So it is no use your saying to me: "Concentration is difficult; I shall never be able to accomplish it."   I know how easy it is, and how easy for you as well as for me, though it is not so easy to remove your unfaith.   A little child might say, "I cannot walk," but mother holds open her arms and says, "Come on, come on," and the child walks, tottering perhaps at first, but later with a free and joyous tread.

So do not tell me you cannot concentrate.   That would be saying that you cannot do anything at all and that you never have done anything with prior thought. Is it in the nature of men to concentrate their minds when they wish to do so or not? Of course it is.   But I know what is the matter with you; you are wishing, not willing.   You have not said: "I will concentrate."   You have not even said: "I will begin to concentrate, just a very little bit."

When you pick up your book what do you say to yourself? First, "Shall I pick up the book?" and then "I will pick up the book."   In this there is no wishing at all.   There is only will, as soon as you know that you *can* lift the book.   But as long as you say to yourself: "I wish I could concentrate; I wish I could concentrate; I wish I could concentrate. . ." you are telling yourself that you cannot do it.   If the book weighed five hundred pounds instead of eight ounces you might say, "I wish I could pick up that book."   That statement would be a true and proper acknowledgment of your inability to do so, and an appropriate obstacle to the formation of the mental picture which precedes the movement of the hand.   As it is, however, you cannot say, "I wish," because you know full well—or, rather, you have faith—

that you *can* pick it up.   So you cannot wish in the matter; you are bound to say, "I will pick it up," or, "I will not pick it up."   And when you have taken one elementary step in concentration you will no longer be able to say: "I wish I could concentrate," because you will know that you can.   You will only be able to say, "I will concentrate," or "I will not concentrate."   It is the first step that counts, and if you will not take the first step you are no use to yourself or to anybody else.

One thing I must say about this.   In your first steps do not judge yourself.   You have to go on without thinking of success or failure.   "Perfection or nothing" is not a good motto for the beginner in any art.

CHAPTER IV

CHAINS OF THOUGHT

THE WALKING MIND

WE have studied the first process of thought—the way in which every idea opens out in many directions. We have now to consider the second process—the way in which our attention passes on from one idea to another and forms a flow of thought. It is a matter almost of common knowledge that our attention travels among thoughts very much in the same way as our body moves about among things. So close is the similarity that we may say that the attention seems actually to walk on two feet from one mental image or idea to another.

Suppose, for example, I start to think about a cow, and a few moments later I find myself thinking about a curio shop. There is a reason for this, which I can discover by tracing back in memory the series of preceding thoughts. Before "curio shop" there was a picture of some old artistic glassware; before that was "glass", before that "bottle", before that "milk-bottle"—and so back to "milk" and "cow".

What is to be noticed now is not so much the procession of memories as the series of forgettings. Every operation of memory includes an act of forgetting many other things; what remains after the forgetting is in the focus of consciousness and is called a memory. Thus, "cow" and "milk" stand together in one compound natural picture. My attention contains both "cow" and "milk" at one moment. They are part of a unit idea. Next, "cow" is set aside or forgotten and "milk" connects with "bottle" and produces one unit composed of "milk" and "bottle," that is, milk in a bottle. There is not a unit "cow and bottle"; such a unit would be a less familiar and more unstable compound idea. It will not arise in the flow of ideas thrown up by subconscious association, but would require an act of will (such as we are using now) to produce and hold it, and the least slackening of that will would result in the breaking up of that compound picture, it being deficient in unity.

Here let me refer to modern art. If in a picture various things presented together are not in the familiar groupings of nature, the whole is unpleasing though the parts taken separately may be very pleasing. We all feel there is no beauty in such a combination, though we may not all understand the reason for it, which is that beauty is the mind's delight in unity. We shall probably call it a restless picture. But we must remember that in the coterie of artists who enjoy those pictures, and can enjoy them for a long time, there is a background of mental habits which have lingered upon an obscure relationship between those odd parts and have made them familiar associates in such special workings of the mind, outside the experience of ordinary men.

We see now that the flow of thoughts, or rather ideas, in the course of ordinary mental drift or day-dreaming is due to subconscious associations, which in their turn were originally formed by conscious observation and thinking. It is analogous to body processes such as walking. There is, as I have already mentioned, a very close resemblance to the use of two legs in walking.

There are seven stepping stones between my kitchen entrance and the tool room. Call them A to G. I have my left foot on A and my right foot on B and I am on the move, or, in other words, I have inherent momentum. My left foot lifts off A, swings over to C and plants itself there, and then my right foot lifts from B and moves on to D, and so my body is carried along on what seems a continuous movement, which however consists also of a series of stoppages on resistant stepping-stones. The successive ideas in the mind are like the stepping-stones, among which B is contiguous to A and C, and F is contiguous to E and G, but A is not contiguous to C, nor E to G.

Now another point. I could if I wished stop and stand on one stepping-stone. Or poise my attention on one of the ideas—say milk. If I concentrate on milk and do not go on to bottle nor back to cow, milk will begin to give up its secrets—or, it will sprout all its adjacent associations in accordance with the explanation I have already given in connection with the Four Roads of Thought. Perhaps there will be a hundred of those arrows. The more there are the better, for they bring me nearer to knowing what milk really is, that is, to understanding it. The quick and ready associations will be such as baby, calf, cat, cream, butter, cheese, water, liquidity, white colour, goat's milk, cocoanut milk, etc. More obscure ones will arise according to my special knowledge.

If now I cease my concentration the drift will begin again, beginning with any one of the arrows. Consideration of this will show us how at every moment there is a choice—a fork in the road of thought. The parting of the ways is small, but soon they are far asunder—a fact which shows how much my future depends upon every step in my thought. It is no wonder that the ancient psychologists of India, holding that what a man thinks determines what he will become, developed a system of mental exercises, termed Raja Yoga, calculated to speed men swiftly onwards to the fulfilment of human life in the perfection of mind, and its full opening to those spiritual realities which it only very dimly perceives in the case of the average person at the present time.

A diagram will show us the divergence of the thought-streams:

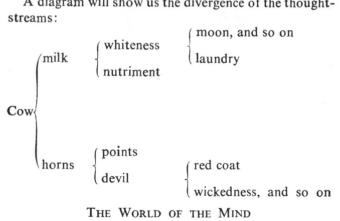

THE WORLD OF THE MIND

The human body has been described as a vehicle for carrying a bag of tools. I sent for a California carpenter the other day. He arrived in an ancient Ford, from which he brought out a very modern kit-box containing at least a hundred tools. In the human body we find legs with which to carry the rest of the outfit about, arms to work with and alter the world, and senses to see what those things are. This carpenter operates in an immense world, but attends to a very small part of it—he sees only a small portion, and works only on a bit of that.

The world is full of a number of things—as somebody mildly expressed it. The senses at any moment present a quantity of these to me. I cannot grasp all these at once, but to have clarity and sanity I must confine my attention to only a very few of them. Here at my writing table, if I lean back, I see shelves bearing books in English and books in Sanskrit, iron document boxes, cardboard envelope boxes, bundles of papers—lecture notes, letters, bills (all paid, permit me to say)—spare office tools such as pencils and clips, a door with locks and handles, a window with all its glass and wood and hardware, and through its glass, some trees outside, and just beyond them thousands of red and green and white lights of Hollywood, spread out below, and further away the light haze of the City of Los Angeles reflecting itself in the evening sky, where too, there are some moving lights of aeroplanes and swinging beams of searchlights turned up into the atmosphere. Within the window there are still other things: walls, ornaments, pictures. Immediately in front is my writing table with a litter (my wife says it is untidy, but I say it is only a contiguity!) of papers, books, letters, pens, pencils, inkstand, rubbers, scissors, stamps, glasses, and pleasing to relate, some money, though not too much. I see also—I nearly forgot this—some part of the floor beneath and near the table, with carpets, waste basket and—I confess it—some papers to both right and left thrown into grocery cartons on the floor, awaiting my attention.

Oh, what a lot of things. And what varied and multitudinous stories each one of them could tell. I think I could write about them for a thousand years without rising from this chair—yet I have spoken only of what my eyes bring to me. There is hearing too—the ticking of the clock, the distant sounds of motor-cars, and a faint barking of dogs, sounds of someone moving and making culinary noises in the kitchen about fifty feet away, and some singing in my ears (now I think of it). I have not spoken of smell and touch, but in the latter field there is the feel of the pen in my hand, my forearms on the edge of the table, my behind on the seat of the chair, and, almost all over, various small sensations related to clothing—when I attend to them—from shoes to shirt. I feel my eyes blinking, my nose tickling, and, verily, a faint creaking in my unmoving joints.

And I—poor little fellow—must miss most of this wealth of life and story, look at a sheet of paper, and allow my hand to trace signs thereon in obedience to a flow of ideas.

Ideas! Ah, there is another of those worlds. We call it an inner world of the mind. Is it a world? Who knows? I seem to pluck ideas and often even new knowledge from some inner world. It does not appear that I make them, but rather that I see them. I find it hard to credit to my own thinking or memory many of these ideas. Looking thus at what is taking place in what I call my life within my mind, I see that there is a great similarity to the world of the senses called the outer world.   Here also I am looking and picking among a great quantity of objects.   As I have travelled about in the material world and at every moment been confronted by a myriad of objects all spreading a table of riches before me, uprising from the minds and actions of all living beings, with all their uncharted riches, so also it seems as if I have travelled in a world of ideas—as thick and numerous and as infinitely various as objects of the material world, and that all the time I am only looking and picking, looking to pick and picking to look, and I am only the looker-on at all these things and thoughts.

It is as if there were a vast region of true ideas, some of which I now know through the instrumentality of my mind, but most of which remains for me the apparently unlimited unknown.   In that world also I have a vehicle, albeit unmoving; by my will it "travels about" in the world of thought, pursues a course of mental life, just as my body lives and moves about in the outer world. That vehicle is the mind, the focus of my consciousness for mental things.   Let us take another simile and say that this mental body, in which I am able to attend to ideas, is like a little fish swimming about in a vast ocean of ideas, and there seeing and informing me of what comes within the range of its limited faculties.   It cannot see beyond a short range; it cannot leap through space; it must travel through intermediate points to pass from one place to another, from one idea to another.

THE TRACK OF THE FISH

Be it folly or wisdom, I must concentrate on some part of this world.   Few men have the inclination and

power to ignore it altogether. I must decide to pay attention to this thing or idea rather than that. For this
purpose it is the little fish of attention that I have to
control.

Put this matter to yourself. You want the fish to
(1) Swim in the direction you have chosen, and (2) ex-
tend and improve its range of vision, its ability to present before you fully and clearly the events with which
it meets as it travels through the world of thought. The
concentration practised already will have improved its
vision; now we have to deal with its power to travel. As
the attention passes from object to object in this mental
scene it finds no limit; its horizon for ever recedes as it
approaches it.

THE POWER OF THE MOOD

Amidst all this competition for my attention what is
it that causes me to pick up this or that? Briefly, it is
the mood of the mind. We know that the will can step
into the current of thoughts, watch them drifting along,
and interrupt and direct them. We have seen that it
can also impose an overall command or give standing
orders covering a period of time.

This is true not only regarding the mood of concentration, but for other moods also. You can have a
general hook-up on a particular subject, so that, if it is
architecture, for example, your thought of an elephant
will pass on to its structure, mechanical balance and the
harmonious appearance of its parts, or your thought of
groceries will lead direct to market buildings. But if
you were a woodsman in Burma, "elephant" would lead

to a picture of the carrying and loading of timber in the forests, or if you were a house-wife " groceries " would lead on to thoughts of feeding the family. There are habitual moods produced by our occupations, hobbies, health, social conditions, strong desires and aversions, hopes and fears. Some advertisers of merchandise know something of this, and seek to produce in the public mind moods towards their special products, which they cunningly associate with objects we already like. Thus a pretty picture of father, mother and child, young and well dressed and pleasantly smiling, and sitting in affectionate attitudes in a beautiful, spacious, well-furnished room will connect your home-building mood with somebody's brand of carpets. Mr. Stargazer, the astronomer, however, will be no fish for this net.

Consider how different are the experiences of an architect, a humorist and a doctor, walking arm-in-arm along a city street. The first notices the form and structure of the buildings, the second sees the idiosyncrasies of the passers-by, the third cannot miss the jaundiced eye, the sagging cheek in this one, the strong shoulders and well-sprung gait in that. Each sees, and afterwards uses, what the others do not see. Each unconsciously selects. And further, each is brought to the event that concerns him most. Concentration will make you see and use what concerns you, and further your end.

Words can often give us a clue to moods. Long ago people made a game of this. I call out a word and ask the members of the party to write down the first thought coming into their minds. My word is "links", and I receive "chain" from Alf, who is a surveyor, "cuff-links" from Bert, who is a bit of a dandy, "golf" from Charlie, who is seriously devoted to the game, "torch" from Dick, who is fond of reading about life in the Middle Ages of Europe, and "puma" from Ed, the naturalist, who thought I had said "lynx". Not to leave the girls out of it, I now pronounce the word "foundation" and Ada comes out with "concrete," which is quite explicable when we know she is in the architecture class at College. As most people know, something similar to this is often used as a probe in mental pathology.

POLARIZATION OF THOUGHT

It remains to be said that we can deliberately cultivate a mood by concentrating upon it, and thus can predispose the mind to certain associations of thought, so that whatever may turn up in the world or in the mind will lead on to our purpose. This is the way in which concentration leads to success in our chosen vocation or avocation. It makes almost everything you meet a co-worker of yours. Things coming within your purview are polarized by this, so that your experience is unified and you gain both knowledge and power. Or, if you have several purposes or pieces of work, you can turn from one to another when necessary with clear cut precision by switching over your mood.

I will now give an exercise in the polarization of thought:

Exercise 4. I pick the following subjects at random by casually opening a dictionary. The first word I light upon is "tranquillity", the second "masticate", the third "hexagon," and the fourth "deep". We will suppose you are going to concentrate and perhaps meditate on tranquillity, so as to understand and feel it better than you have done before, and we will suppose that you have come upon the ideas "masticate," "hexagon" and "deep" and you want them to be polarized to "tranquillity". The following are specimen operations, but you should also make your own:

(1) Think of mastication, with tranquillity in view as the goal of a mental series. Your thought must bridge the gap between these two, like an electric spark between two carbons. Hold on till you get the connection. Do not give up. Something will come; never mind if it seems silly. Here is one that comes to me: mastication —no toothache—tranquillity. That would come from someone who had been having dental treatment to remove pain. Here is another: mastication—good digestion—good sleep—tranquillity. There must be plenty more.

Now (2) Hexagon. Repeat the word, and look mentally at a hexagon with tranquillity in view. My first thought is that the hexagon is a well-balanced figure, well-poised, giving me a tranquil feeling which I could not so easily receive from a lop-sided diagram. Then, too, to me a hexagon suggests the familiar symbol of the interlaced triangles, which is interpreted by many symbologists as the harmonious or balanced union of the triple mind (will, love and thought) with the triple world (matter, force and law), instead of the very symbol of tranquil power.

Now (3) Deep. "Still waters run deep." Also deep thoughts make for tranquillity.

Use your own dictionary to get new words with which to experiment, and make your own connections for daily practice for a week.

CHAPTER V

CONCENTRATION IN DAILY LIFE

Outward and Inward Success

CONCENTRATION is not an end in itself, but a means to develop the will so that it may make the entire life purposeful. Polarize your entire life—all your actions, your feelings, your thinking—by establishing a permanent mood towards success in some line of human endeavour. It may be the mood of an artist, a scientist, a poet, a philosopher, a philanthropist; it may concern art, religion, science, interpretation, philosophy, thoughts and deeds of affection and kindness, or works of commerce or government; it may aim at skill in action, or intense and expanded feeling, or a clear and deep understanding of life; it may seek self-government, or, the mastery of environment and success in outward things. That is for you to choose; but choose something definite and polarize your whole life to that.

Polarization of your life-work means that you will have a purpose in life—I do not say a goal, for there is danger in that. One makes a special and often exhausting effort to that end, reaches it and has not the resilience left to go further, so may then linger at that roadside goal for a very long time. That is perhaps one reason why in the *Bhagavad Gita* the aspiring Arjuna is told that his business is with the action only, never with the result of action. To dwell upon the result is to glorify something still very fleeting, or even to block the way to a higher attainment by aiming too low. In this business of living it is function we have to choose, and perfect action is possible within that function every living moment. If I am planting a tree I must give myself fully to the planting, with only a background thought to the apples or oranges that I shall get from the tree a few years hence. Dwelling in thought upon that result will spoil in some measure, perhaps in great measure, my work and my pleasure of planting and the great benefit I can have from that, and even my reverence for work itself and the spiritual values of daily life.

Choose at least one thing in life—a hobby of study or of art if you cannot get into a congenial form of livelihood. Keep up one thing year after year, and gradually you will become a master of that and will find that you possess a personal instrument in which you can enjoy power. Do not despise personality and say it is low and an obstacle to realization of a deeper self. The deeper self will reveal itself through the use of a definite personality, which should have precise form and function in society, and be an instrument for skill in action. Personality is the key to success; it is our box of tools.

There is no real success without goodness, and there is no greatness without goodness. These are not pious sentiments, but material and psychological facts, simply because the alternative to goodness is selfishness—a form of shrinking from life—and the result of dependence upon outward things, which indicates a narrowness or weakness of character. Outward success without inward success is frail and short-lived, like that of men who make money and then fall ill through self-indulgence. It is not only a question of self-indulgence. You cannot be calm and strong if your success depends upon position, power, dignity and security for your own personal self. Your eagerness to have such outward things would mark your dependence upon them, and that dependence would open you up to anxiety about them, and to agitation and distress as they come and go. There is thus no greatness without goodness as well, no outward success without the inward success of a strong will full of goodwill towards others. Outward success without inward strength is an illusion.

Success depends upon what you seek and how you seek. If you have said that you will succeed in anything, you will without fail, no matter how lofty the aim, if your will is in accord with the principle of goodness or unity, the essential law of life. If it is not, you cannot really will; you are only attracted by something outside, and filled for the time being with a ruling desire.

If what you seek is the idle satisfaction of the body or of the senses, or even of the mind, you cannot really say: "I will," for you are the slave of the pleasures of the lower life and you will be drawn wherever the objects of the senses may lead. But if you say: "I will have power;

I will have love; I will have knowledge," you must choose the right way to seek it, and provide that others also are more powerful and freer because you are so, that they have more love because you have much to give, that they have more knowledge because it has come to you.   A rich man living among poor men is not really rich—that is an illusion.   If in pride you hold and withhold power, in order to feel your supremacy over others, you are not obeying the true law of life, you are a slave to the base emotion of pride.   If in your seeking of knowledge your aim is to shine and feel superior, or if you seek love of others for yourself, that you may multiply yourself in them, that they may think well of you and speak highly of you and be drawn to seek your company, once more you are disobeying the true law of life, and are a slave to the base emotion of pride.   And that pride, when thwarted by the accidents of life, will be turned into envy, jealousy, anger and fear, and you will be torn by the conflicting winds of circumstances, drowned in the ocean of wishes, and unable to say: "I will." [1]

Even more will this be so if you seek the satisfaction of the senses or the luxuries of the body; then indeed you will be a slave.   Corrupted with wishes and regrets, there will be no peace and power within you.   Indeed, you must train all your vehicles—your body, feelings and mind—to orderly activity, removing from them all traces of sloth and heaviness, agitation and excitement of every kind, so that they will be perfect instruments

[1] There is perhaps nothing more distressing to have than the superiority complex.   How it should sadden us to think of all these millions of people as below us, and to contemplate the long and painful road that they must tread to reach our eminence.

for carrying out your will in the regions in which they work.

The first thing to do is to select the mood that you will have; then eliminate all those things that can agitate the mind in any way. You must try to get rid of every trace of anger, irritation, anxiety, uncertainty and fear. When such qualities are allowed in the mind there can be no real exercise of will, no real permanence of mood. Success in the practice of mind-control is dependent upon steadiness of mood, and if you are still so infantile in character as to be swayed to anger, anxiety and fear by the so-called accidents of life, you cannot until you command yourself have anything better than shifting moods and a wandering mind. Only the things that are pure and good and kind and calm can be permanent; pride, anger and fear and all their kin are of the essence of agitation and impermanence. Therefore the mood you select must be compatible with your best and most unselfish ideal—unselfish not only for yourself but also for others. You can no longer regard life as a battle with others or for a few others, nor desire to control others; if your aim is the gradual mastery of self and the full development of your powers, your only possible attitude towards others, to all and all the time, is that of a benevolent intention to share with them the freedom and power that you are winning for yourself.

THE FOLLY OF WISHING

Then you must give up wishing, for you cannot both wish and will. The two things are utterly incompatible.

I have already explained this by reference to the will to pick up or not pick up a pen. It should be understood that indulgence in wishing is not only a waste of time, but also an invitation to harmful emotions. It is like slouching along the road instead of walking erect. The only proper attitude of the positive soul towards things, events and people is to accept them for what they are—not wishing them to be different—and then decide what to do about the matter. I am not confusing wanting with wishing. As a result of calm judgment and not of mere wish you can want to have something or to do some act. Even when you have said, "I want this," again you ask, "Do I?" And the wanting that comes out of this thoughtful intuitive poise will be a clear strong feeling, usable for polarization of a mood.[1]

This matter of calm judgment is important, so I will introduce it with a statement, illustrate it with a diagram and elucidate it with a question.

1. *The statement.* Impressions from the outside (through hearing, touch, sight, taste, smell or telepathy) strike upon us, and we react to them *after* they have penetrated into us to a certain depth. These processes are called afferent and efferent by some psychologists. There is a point, however, where the afferent ceases and the efferent begins, and in that I am or you are.

[1] Lest there be any misunderstanding let me make it perfectly clear that wanting includes what are called little things. " I like to wear silk next my skin," says someone. " Do you want it?" I ask. " Do I?—Yes. I do," is the reply. " Good, then, if it harmonizes with your general purpose." It is not a little thing—there are none. That silk is touching your very soul, and to its depths, beyond the depth of which you are so far aware. Quality, not quantity or size, concerns the soul or self.

2. *The diagram.*

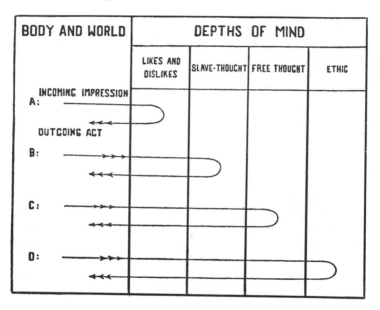

BODY AND WORLD	DEPTHS OF MIND			
	LIKES AND DISLIKES	SLAVE-THOUGHT	FREE THOUGHT	ETHIC
A: INCOMING IMPRESSION				
OUTGOING ACT				
B:				
C:				
D:				

A, represents an animal which reacts from emotional habit; B, the animal-man who does the same with the addition of memory, imagination and cunning; C, the man-man who considers what likes and dislikes to encourage, in accord with "natural law"; D, the godman, or philosopher, who feels for others, and reacts from the depth of intelligent love, or intelligence in service to love. For those who do not immediately see this as a natural and necessary fact, I will merely quote Emerson's statement, to be reflected upon: "I see that when souls reach a certain clearness of perfection, they accept a knowledge and motive above selfishness. A breath of Will blows eternally through the universe of souls in the direction of the Right and Necessary. It is the air which all intellects inhale and exhale, and it is the wind which blows the world into order and orbit." This contains something of a still deeper depth, of which the god-man will become aware in due course—a spiritual intuition of the purpose of our being in the present moment, as though the future tree were talking to the seed or at least the seedling. Enough said. I hope we shall all experience this before too long.

I must prevent a possible error by pointing out that we are not to become dessicated men, without likes and dislikes. We have flesh and blood and a heritage of emotions and ideas; but impressions from all these will be carried inwards on the afferent stream and dealt with according to their true worth as seen in the depths, and brought out again in full strength, but purified.

(3) *The question*. In which depth will you establish your mood? I beg you to think again and again about this, and to explore and re-explore those depths until they become familar ground. Give yourself leisure for thought.

Be brave, then, and face the world with clear thoughts, intelligent love, and enlightened will.

There will be a new policy in your life. Consider it practically. What will it mean to you when you rise in the morning, when you eat, when you lie down to sleep? What when you meet your companions, your friends, your so-called enemies? What when you lose your appointment or money or meet with an accident, or fall ill, and your family suffers? Sit down, and think over the disagreeable things that might happen within the next week, and see in each case what it would mean to you. You would not wish them to be otherwise; you would say to each of them: "What are you for; what use can I make of you?" You would not sink down weeping; nor rise up in thoughtless battling. There is not hoping in this mood—but there is certainty, inherent steadiness of power. There is no expectation, but there is knowledge. There is no fear, but confidence in the true law of life within you and in all things.

Every morning for a week, before you begin the day, spend five minutes in thinking over this strong outlook upon life. Every night before you go to rest, spend a few minutes in glancing back to see how you have maintained your spiritual dignity during the past day. Do not ask yourself especially: "In what have I erred?" but: "In what have I succeeded?" Each day will tell its tale of achievement. Do not wish, nor regret, nor hope. But when you are about to go to sleep, whisper gently: "I will." And when you wake whisper gently: "I will."

ECONOMY OF FORCE

Many people do not realize that it is the nature of man to modify his environment, not to submit to it except in so far as his own judgment advises him to do so. He has the combinative and constructive power of mind which, acting through his hands, alters and adapts old forms and makes new ones by rearranging and combining them.

Just as he is not built with the capacity to attend to everything that strikes his senses, but is well advised to give full and proper attention to a part of it, so he is not able to alter the whole of it at any time. He has to decide what part of his environment he will accept as it is and what part he will alter. "It is raining today. I accept that. Those things in the attic are still dusty and untidy. I will alter that." What-not-to-alter and what-to-alter, and what-to-try-to-alter-although-I-am-not-sure-of-success are the three problems that face us every day. Ask them on rising in the morning. They will help to polarize your day and make it clear, strong and fruitful, because it is the nature of man to use thought in all his works.

"But surely we are not to work all the time?" a rather dismayed voice seems to say. No, clearly we do not live to work, and equally clearly working is not living. What then is living? It is a state of consciousness which exists behind and between the acts of mental and physical work. I will venture to say it is a pure sense of being, filled with happiness. It is only for this that we go on trying and trying. We feel a little of it, even amidst the confusion of daily life. We bear all our pains for the sake of this. Stop the confusion, then pains will diminish and this true state of happy being will more and more be known.

I said "behind and between". There is such a thing as fruitful leisure, when you relax body, emotions and mind. In the triple relaxation the joy of true living can be experienced. You may relax your body quite well, but if the emotions are calling for excitement ("I wish I had a good story to read") or the mind goes on planning, you are still at work. "But," says the troubled voice again. "I would be asleep." No; in such voluntary relaxation you need not become negative; remain positive and you will enjoy a new experience. The old books of India call it by a very long name, but I do not advise anyone to assume or feel that it is beyond his or her reach on that account.   Rather avoid any teacher who tries to instil occult timidity into you, and remember the old saying that he who aims high may rise above mediocrity, but he who aims at mediocrity is likely to fall below it.

It is "behind" as well as "between," because once it is known it will be found to be there even when work of mind and body are going on.   Our present consciousness will thus begin to drop into the role of subconscious to that new consciousness, and we shall then understand how all the life-urges are subconscious workings of our own inherent divine wisdom.

The kind of mental and physical work which leads towards and finally permits this experience is that which shows economy of force.   Watch out for idle thoughts, emotions and actions—they are signs of something to be righted.   Put an end to them more by understanding than by mere suppression, from which they tend to produce a kind of fuming inside.   The child swings its legs. Mother says "Don't".   The child does the "don'ting" instead, and its agitation is now within.

With us, thought and action are to be unified.   Resolve to think no thoughts without reference to action or intended action, and to perform no conscious actions without intention.   This will lead to the cessation of waste of force.

As regards *idle action*, avoid the small wasteful activities and mannerisms in which people often thoughtlessly or nervously indulge.   There is somewhere a story about a member of parliament in London who always fiddled with one of his coat buttons when he was speaking. One day, when a vital issue was at stake, an opponent quietly cut away the button, and thus completely spoiled the speech of his adversary, even though it had been well prepared. That is an extreme case, but ordinarily people fail to acquire poise as long as they permit small movements such as swinging one leg over the other knee, and phrases such as "You see," and "Of course." If you are talking it is better to pause in silence looking for words than to say, "Er-er-er." Every action or word should have a purpose behind it. The larger wasteful activities must also be proscribed, such as lying in bed late in the morning, wasting time at night, eating unnecessary food, struggling to obtain things which are not really required, and the wasteful activity of unnecessary and irrelevant work. Also bodily excitement and nervous and muscular tension are to be avoided as far as possible. These wasteful habits are difficult to change suddenly, and it is better to make a resolution to operate for an hour daily and carry it out, gradually increasing the time, than to resolve to change every useless habit at once and fail to carry out the resolution.

As regards *idle thought*, do not go over and over the same argument. If there is to be a decision—shall we go to the mountains or the sea for our holidays?—and the pros and cons seem equal, it does not matter much which way is decided upon. You may even settle that by tossing a coin. The same rule applies even to weightier matters. Sometimes, however, immediate action is not imperative, and decision can be suspended to await the arrival of additional data or to let the matter settle itself. Quiet suspension of decision is itself also a form of decision; it is the decision what to do now.   Practise the habits of voluntary decision and voluntary suspension of thought.

In this practice you can make use of what are often troubles, and even enjoy them—such troubles as delayed business, and personal clashes. Think them over; think them out.   " How much truth is there in that disagreeable statement? What ought to be done in these circumstances, and what can be done? Is this worth attention at all?" Think first, then decide.   First decide to think, then decide whether to decide or to suspend decision.

There remains still the removal of *idle emotions*. The seeking of small pleasures which are not creative, and the indulgence in emotion without its corresponding action and thought are weakening to the will. Your chief purpose should be your chief pleasure—if it is not so, either the purpose or the pleasure is unhealthy.

True Work is Play

When purpose and pleasure are brought together work becomes play. Every bit of work done in this spirit strengthens the man who does it. It is recreative as well as creative. Artist and carpenter—they make pictures and chairs, but even more they make men, themselves. Think on what you are doing more than on the result, or what you are going to do afterwards. You will not then miss the pleasure of little things. I pick up my pen; there is a sheer and undiluted pleasure in this, if I allow myself to experience it. It is natural and pure, and mine when I stop fighting it. In such little things thought, love and will can flow and grow

And then arise peace and strength and—in active life—the union of work and play.

Moderation is another law. Play ceases to be play when there is fatigue or overstrain. We have much to learn from the animals and even from the plants in this respect. "Grow as the flower grows," says *Light on the Path*, "opening your heart to the sun." Said Jesus: "Consider the lilies of the field; they toil not, neither do they spin; and yet I say unto you that Solomon in all his glory was not arrayed like one of these." It is deadly fear of the morrow that makes man's work a toil, that makes him sweat in bitterness. But the law of life says: "Do the wise and right thing to-day, and leave the result to take care of itself." This is not a doctrine of idleness, but of work that is play instead of toil.

An illustration of this is to be seen in the way in which different people take a long journey. One man will get into the train and remain in a fever of impatience until he reaches his destination. He has fixed his mind on something that he wants to do there; in the meantime his journey is a toil and a misery. Another knows how to use and enjoy the scenery, the people and even the train itself.

These thoughts bring up in my mind two contrasting pictures. I see a Western man sitting on his tractor moving along a field. He does not seem to be enjoying his work. Perhaps he is thinking of something else—of going to a dance or a cinema. He has been educated in a practical way but not for the understanding of life and enjoyment of the common day.

I see a Hindu villager tilling a field. I know what is in his mind. He is perhaps singing to himself one of the old songs. He is thinking of the earth and the water that waters the earth, and he loves them both with every nerve of his body. If he were a kissing man he would kiss them, but he belongs to a devotional race, so he salutes them, and touches them with a feeling that he is being blessed. He looks at the grass banks which border his field. Along their narrow tops he will walk away from his work at eventide. He will walk without shoes, and his feet will feel and respond to the irregularities of the path. As he comes to each border-tree on that path he will feel happy, as though he had met a friend whom he does not fear. And so he will come at last, without hurry, to his earth-walled and palm-roofed home, where his wife and children live, and where his fathers before him have lived, perhaps for a thousand years.

But perhaps I have misjudged that Western man. Perhaps he is thinking not of dance and cinema, but how when he reaches his home in the evening he will go out and work in the garden for a while, touching the soil and the little plants, with a slightly busy wife and toddling child near by—away from the deadly constructiveness of his daily work, which even when it gives him elation does not give him joy, into some simple living with life.

It may be said that I have taken extreme cases of West and East in my contrasting picture. Yes, that is so, yet there is something in it in general, and undoubtedly we human beings will have to bring work and play together for both our individual and our social redemptions.

The Four Great Enemies

It is said in an old Indian book that there are four great enemies to human success: (1) a sleepy heart,

(2) human passions, (3) a confused mind, and (4) attachment to anything but Brahman.[1]

A sleepy heart—means that the body is lazy and its activities are slothful.

Human passions—means that the emotions are only reactions from pleasure and pain.

A confused mind—means one that still lacks the wisdom-knowledge that gives it constancy or unity of purpose.

In mastering all these you must not aim at repression or destruction, but at well-regulated activity, that is, culture. Physical culture involves the suppression of irregular activities in the body. It demands an ordered life, with well-proportioned exercise, nourishment and rest. The governing of the natural appetites which it requires does not nullify their power, but tunes them up; and the sense of vigorous life is increased, not diminished by this control.

These things are true also of the mind. It too requires regular and well-proportioned exercise, nourishment and rest. Its natural appetites also need to be controlled and governed, and when this is done there is no loss of mental vigour, but an enhancement of it.

Exercise is something more than the mere use of faculty. A man breaking stones on the road is using his muscles, and certainly in a long time the muscles he uses become strong. A man who carries out a definite system of physical exercises for a short time every day soon becomes stronger than the man who wields the

---

[1] Each student has to attach his own meaning to this word, keeping it always flexible, so that it may expand and become illumined. Literally: the Evolutioner, Grower or Expander, not creator.

hammer all day long. So also, a man who spends his time in the study of mathematics, literature, languages, science, philosophy, or any other subject, is using his mind, and thinking may become facile to him. But a man who deliberately carries out a definite system of mental exercises for a short time every day, soon gains greater control of his mind than he who merely reads and curiously thinks all day long.

In fact, the need of mental training, of regular, orderly, purposeful exercise of the mind, is far greater than that of the body in most cases; for at our general stage of growth most men's bodily activities are well-ordered and controlled, and the body is obedient to their will, but their minds are usually utterly disobedient, idle and luxurious.

In the next chapter of this book various exercises for the body are prescribed. These are intended to regulate and calm it. Calmness does not mean dullness or immobility. It means regular motion and is quite compatible with rapid motion. So also control of mind does not mean dullness or stupidity. It means clear-cut and regular thought, velocity and strength of mind, vivid and living ideas.

Without the preliminary training which makes the body calm, control of mind is difficult. A certain small measure of austerity is imperatively necessary for great success in concentration. The reason for this is to be discovered in the basic rule of the process. That rule is this: the body must be still, the mind alert.

Determined perseverance does not usually walk hand in hand with absence of excitement in human life. Yet for success the mind must be calm. The ideal aimed at should be clearly pictured in the mind, and then kept constantly before it.   Such a prevailing mood will tend to polarize all thought, desire and activity to its direction.   As a traveller may follow a star through mazes of forest and trackless country, so will the persistent ideal guide its votary infallibly through all difficult and complex situations in life.   All that is necessary is constant practice and absence of agitation.

Constant practice and absence of excitement or agitation—these two rules are always prescribed.   Do you not see that they are the natural accompaniments of will? If you have said: "I will," not only in words, but also in act, and thought, and feeling, will you not always be free from the excitement and weakness of wishing?

If thus you work and practise, and never wish, and have no attachment to anything but Brahman, success will soon be yours.   Life will fulfil itself when the obstacles are removed.   In the distant future, do you say? Is it not sure? And what is sure is just as good as if it had already happened; so if you will not have it otherwise, even now success is yours all the time, not only in the end.

CHAPTER VI

CONTROL OF THE BODY AND SENSES

How to Sit

I HAVE already spoken of relaxation and muscle balance, and their relation to the practices of concentration and meditation. These are necessary so that (1) the body may not be injured by the mental efforts and (2) the mental work may not be spoiled by bodily discomfort. Thirdly, we have to remember that bodily attitudes are associated with states of feeling, such as lying down with sleep, and kneeling with prayer. That has to be taken into consideration when you are selecting a posture, but there is no objection to your lying down to concentrate or meditate, so long as you find that it does not conduce to sleepiness.

Try to select an attitude for concentration which will be free from disturbing associations. It is generally found advantageous to sit upright with the eyes closed, the hands resting, and the head and neck straight but not stiff.

You will probably find that the body is not as obedient as you would like it to be. It is often restless and im-patient or troubled by trifling sensations, even when you have removed any causes of discomfort that there may be. Do not permit this. The body must be your servant. Will you be master? Raise yourself up, and say: "I will." Do not wish, but say: "I will." If the body is not bright and obedient, train it. To-morrow, and each day for one month set aside some time every day and do the following exercises.

1. Standing still.
2. Nerve exercise.
3. Relaxing.
4. Breathing exercises.
5. Stretching and bending exercises.

Do all these faithfully every day for one month. If you miss one day begin again on the next and then do the exercises for one full month without missing once. This will give you an opportunity of doing something that is at once beneficial to the body and valuable training for the will. Train your body as a fancier would train a prize dog; do not starve it or beat it, but do not indulge it harmfully. If you find that under this new regime old dirt comes to the surface, and the body becomes weak and ill—an effect due to past indulgence. not to present strain—stop the practice for a few days. Then begin all over again, and thus go on again and again until the body is sound, clean and strong. Continue until weakness and sluggishness disappear. If necessary, make a change in your diet, in the direction of the "cheerful" foods. avoiding both "heavy" and "exciting" things.

THE FIVE BODILY EXERCISES

1. *The Standing Exercise.* With your watch in sight try to stand perfectly still (except for breathing and

blinking) in front of a mirror for three to five minutes. Make no response to any twitching, tickling, itching, creeping, aching or creaking feelings that may arise. Think "stillness," not "not-moving-ness."

2. *Nerve Exercise.* Sit down with your elbow resting and hand raised, and look intently at the palm and fingers, keeping them quite still. Very soon you may feel creeping sensations in the muscles and a tingling in the finger-tips, with a sensation of something flowing off. Something does flow off, and has even been photographed occasionally during the last fifty years; but now observe that you can reverse the flow by an act of will. Send it back up the arm. Let it flow and reverse it several times, keeping the hand quite still.

Afterwards practise this without looking, for both hands and feet, and use the mood of it to reverse the currents at times when you may become excited by unusually "nervous occasion". I call it "nerve-fluid continence". There may be times, however, when you will feel this flow—perhaps even in floods—and some intuition will instruct you to let it go, and some other intuition may even tell you where it is going.

3. *The Relaxing Exercises.* The first part of this work is to acquire the feel of relaxation, for which I recommend the following. Hold one arm out in front about level with the shoulder, loosely, with the elbow a little bent and the hand drooping from the wrist. With the other hand hold a book, edge upwards under the forearm, and try to find the pivotal point of the horizontal arm, so as to get it well balanced on the book. When you are satisfied that the arm will rest balanced on the book without falling, use your imagination to relax it

progressively from the finger-tips, thinking the withdrawal of energy slowly into the shoulder. When the arm feels relaxed, suddenly pull away the book. The arm should fall lifeless, if it is relaxed. (You could treat this as a game on some occasions, getting a second person to hold the book and pull it away unexpectedly.) Try this several times, as you may not at first achieve the required mental feeling, on which follows the physical obedience.

Once you have caught the feeling of relaxation practise it lying down. Stretch yourself progressively, beginning with the toes and feet and legs, then up the trunk, fingers and arms also, to the neck—stretch the neck especially, wriggling it about and entirely loosening it (this is very important)—chin, lips, cheeks and nose, brow, and scalp. As you proceed, let each part in turn sink back into relaxation, until at the completion of the process you give a sigh of physical pleasure which empties your lungs, which then quite naturally start breathing again in a gentler manner and with a slower tempo than before. Now you should feel a cat-like luxury, with a complete disinclination to rise.

4. *Breathing Exercise.* Thin, shallow breathing does not conduce to mental power any more than to bodily health. Strong, slow, quiet, steady breathing is best, and again we need to establish a mood for the concentration-breath, which can be put on and taken off like a garment. For both strength and control, first become diaphragm-conscious. Singers and speakers do this in various ways. One of the best is first to find the diaphragm by placing your hand just below your ribs and above your waist in front and then panting through your

mouth like a dog.   Pant until your muscles ache.   Next, sitting easily erect, neither relaxed nor taut, put your mind on the front of the chest, not in the middle, but towards the sides, and, simply by thinking and will, not by breathing, produce a series of slight feelings of expansion and contraction of the chest, not so much forward as diagonally sideways.   After a little practice you can control these muscles by thought.

Now you are equipped to set the mood for concentration-breath.   First breathe out as fully as you can. Next draw the breath in slowly and evenly through both nostrils, depressing the diaphragm, then, keeping the diaphragm down, draw in more air by expanding the chest.   In other words, drink down and fill up in two successive but continuous motions.   Hold the fullness a little while and slowly exhale.   Do not overdo this in any way.   The intention is not to take in more air than is normal when the lungs are reasonably fully used, that is, properly used, but to counteract habits of shallowness, irregularity and excitability.   One thus teaches the body what good breathing feels like, removes the old built-in wrong feeling and replaces it by the new right feeling, which will soon be ignorable, when it sinks into the sub-conscious, becoming a habit.   Do not push the chest out and hollow the back, but rather draw the muscles of the abdomen well in—which straightens and flattens the back—and keep them in while practising any breathing exercises.   Indeed, it is a good thing now and then during the day whether standing, sitting or lying down, to move these muscles up and down a number of times, and finish the exercise with them up, not voluntarily consenting to their dropping at any time.   They can in this way become obedient and strong, so that in connection with breathing well one naturally avoids the error of pushing the chest out, and performs the correct action of drawing the abdominal muscles in. One does not then confuse these muscles with the diaphragm. Do not hold the breath so long that you have to exhale rapidly or explosively. Every one must find for himself the measure for healthy breathing. Slow breathing is conducive to placidity and long life. I think we are all likely to know by the feel of it when to let it go and when to stop it, but have to watch carefully not to mix it with our personal emotions.

Some say you should count, or tell beads—so many units of time for inbreathing, so many for holding the air in the lungs, so many for letting it out. Many old teachers advise a 1, 4 and 2 unit rhythm, but this was for special purposes; probably the average modern person will find about 4, 4, and 4 convenient, with a unit of about 1 second. Quite a good policy is to practise as you feel it easy and pleasant. For the practice of concentration unusual forms of breathing, such as very slow or long breathing and the practice of breathing up one nostril and down the other, are not required; abnormalities and extremes are to be avoided as dangerous. And never cork the breath in at the throat, under the erroneous assumption that you are "holding the breath".

5. *Stretching and Bending Exercises.* After you have done the preceding four exercises, you may do these to put the body in trim for ordinary activities of life. It is well to do them also after any prolonged period of sitting.

Stand with the heels together; raise the hands reaching high above the head; bend forward to touch the toes without bending the knees; return to the upright position, reaching as high as possible, standing on the toes.

Stand as before; let the hands and arms rest straight down the sides, with the backs of the hands turned outwards from the knees; slowly raise the unbent arms outwards and upwards, until the backs of the hands touch above the head; stretch, rising on the toes and looking upwards; slowly return.

Stand once more with the hands at the sides, palms inwards; lean over slowly to one side until the hand sinks below the knee, while the other hand is curled up under the armpit; slowly swing back to the opposite side, stretching the body all the time.

Perform all the exercises with an even movement and concentrated thought, for at least one minute each. Finally stand, raise one foot from the floor by bending the knee; now raise the other and lower the first, and thus run for about a minute, without moving along. In this exercise the two feet do not both touch the ground at the same time. In all these or any other exercises do nothing to strain the heart.

Extras. There are certain exercises for the eyes and neck which can be performed in oddments of time which would otherwise be wasted. Both these organs need a training in balanced musculature. I seem to remember that someone once said: "You are as young as your neck." Perhaps I only thought it. In any case, it is true. For balanced musculature you need development, loosening and relaxation. First stretch your neck to loosen it and let it sink back into place. Then there are six exercises; (1) Rolling the head slowly round and round, both ways; (2) Slowly nodding the head far forwards and backwards; (3) Lolling the head over from one side to the other; (4) Twisting the head to right and left; (5) Jutting the chin out horizontally and bringing it far back without altering the level; (6) Carrying the head a little to the right and left without altering its vertical position. Finally again stretch your neck and loosen it back into place.

Another good exercise for the neck is to sit with your hands on your knees and slowly roll the upper part of the torso round and round, while having the neck completely relaxed, so that the head also rolls round, but only by gravity. Begin this exercise by leaning forward and letting the head loll forward, pulling upon the back of the neck by its weight only, causing a feeling of stretch. Then move the torso round slowly. As the right shoulder goes down, the head, being relaxed, will roll over on that side, and so on right round. This should be done several times, both ways. A good finale, while the head is forward, is to shake the whole relaxed face—not too forcibly—with jaw, lips, nose, temples and all loosely wobbling in their state of relaxedness. Unpleasant as this may appear to any spectator, you will find the effect very pleasing when you restore yourself to your usual equilibrium.

For the eyes, while you sit comfortably without moving your head, let your gaze very slowly and steadily follow the outline of the opposite wall or some large object, first in one direction, then in another. At every decided change of direction close the eyes tightly for a moment. Go up and down, across and diagonally, as well as round and round both ways. As a variant of this exercise, look at a near object and then to something beyond it, in other words, look from near to far and back again, not jerkily, but with slow motion. In general, for eye health, don't sit in a room where you cannot see something twenty feet away, at which you can look whenever you pause for thought, or, if you must be in a small room, learn to "look through the wall." Sometimes children look at the ceiling when the teacher asks a question. Sometimes there then comes an ignorant rebuke: "Look at me, not at the ceiling; you will not find the answer there,"—making it more difficult for the child to think, and perhaps even harming his eyes.

All the foregoing exercises can be practised at any odd spare moments. They will always prove time well spent. So precious are they all that I would say to anyone who feels miserable and depressed: "Just do some of them, and especially the neck exercises, and then see how you feel!"

WHY PHYSICAL EXERCISES?

The question arises: "why should one recommend physical exercises in a course of mental concentration?" The answer is that they are not necessary, but if the student has the time and the will-power they are advisable in order to correct bad habits of breathing, posture and nervous tension. The evolution of the body has taken place under conditions of Nature in which unhealthy, that is inharmonious, features have been discouraged and eliminated, while healthy or harmonious ones have been steadily built up and preserved. But now, modern man uses his body for various kinds of work which produce disproportionate, unbalanced and inharmonious developments and habits, which he will do well to correct by a few special exercises. Nothing that we can do to the body will develop the powers or the maturity of the mind, but bodily disharmony sometimes makes mental exercises difficult. Still, it is better to neglect the body, and work at the maturing of the mind-powers, rather than the reverse.

CONTROL OF SENSATION

At the end of a month of practice of the kind of physical exercises given in this chapter, though you can sit quietly, and the body has become lighter and brighter, so that you can get up like a cat in the morning, you may still find yourself troubled by outside things during concentration or meditation. Noises, for example, may divert you. In that case spare fifteen minutes a day for a month for practice on the following lines.

This is necessary because complete seclusion and quietude are not usually obtainable even for a short time. However fortunate you may be in your circumstances, you cannot escape entirely from light, sound and wind, and other interruptions. This, however, need not matter much, if you train your senses to ignore the records of the sense-organs. When we are deeply engrossed in a book we may be perfectly unaware that birds are singing outside and trees shaking and rustling in the wind, or that the fire is crackling on the hearth and the clock ticking on the mantel-shelf, though these sounds are actually entering the ear and moving the sense-organs. It is not that the ear does not respond to the sounds, but that the senses are turned away from the sense-organs. So also the eyes may be open while we are in a "brown study," and nothing is seen, though the retina contains the image of all things from which light-waves are proceeding to the eye. If the clock suddenly stops, the attention is at once attracted to inquire about the unexpected change; so also if a large cloud suddenly obscures the sun, or a fresh, damp wind strikes the nostrils or the skin. These things would not attract the senses if we were not maintaining within the mind at least a little consciousness of outward things and interest in them. The student must learn to ignore these outside things at will.

The practice is sometimes followed of withdrawing attention from the outer sounds and forms by listening to sounds and attending to lights and feelings within the body. Such sounds as are set up by the movement of air in the ear and other cavities, or by the circulation of the blood, or by other bodily phenomena, are unnoticed in the grosser sounds of life when we are attending to common affairs, but when we sit down silent and inattentive to outer impacts these more delicate impressions may be found in consciousness. These may be chosen as objects of concentration, and when they have displaced the outer sounds they may themselves be forgotten while the entire attention is being given to the object of concentration.

It is a difficult matter to turn the senses away from the sense-organs. Sit quietly and listen intently to the ticking of the clock. Then try not to hear it, first by an effort not to do so, and then by intent attention to something else. Again, try deliberately to confuse the sound by mixing it with others produced by your imagination, and in the confusion lose sight of the original sound.

The best way to rid oneself of such interruptions is to select a place where as little interruption as possible can come, and then remove from the mind all expectancy or interest in outside changes. Consider, before beginning your practice of concentration, whether any physical phenomena concern you for the time being. Do you expect anyone to call you or interrupt you? Do you fear that someone may surprise you in what may seem to the ignorant a ridiculous occupation? Even if you do, it is better to avoid expectancy. Do not be constantly on the listen for someone's coming. All such expectancy keeps the senses vividly attentive to the slightest sound. In short, resolve that during the time of practice anything that may occur in the outer world does not concern you in the least, and that you will pay positively no attention to external matters. If there is an unusual sound, cease to wonder what was the cause of it or what it means. Cease to take interest in outward changes and they will soon drop out of consciousness.

CHAPTER VII

THE REMOVAL OF INTRUDING THOUGHTS

TROUBLE FROM ONESELF

SOMETIMES when we are engaged in study or writing a visitor arrives; he may be a welcome friend at any other time, but at the moment he is a trouble.   So also when we are engaged in an attempt at concentration, "visitors" throng in upon us, some welcome and others unwelcome. What is it that brings them here so inopportunely, and by what means can we persuade them to take their leave?

A little study of these intruding thoughts will show that they are mostly concerned with considerations of self, and are linked to some emotion and memory in the mind.   There is always a tendency for us to regard the things and persons that we meet in the light of how they affect our own lives.   As long as this is so, feelings about them will invade our minds when we least require them, and these emotions in turn will awaken their corresponding trains of thought.

If Colonel Snuffamout is a jolly good fellow to all his companions at the club, he is none the less a rank bully to his hapless subordinates, and any thought of him will arouse emotions of cordiality in the one case and of resentment in the other.   If I take a walk across the

sands, I find the moving particles an insecure and disagreeable foothold; but doubtless the camel finds them
indeed pleasant to the hoof.   It is so with all the events
of life; each thing has its agreeable and its disagreeable
aspects, and the latter will end for you only when we
have learned to use them all to further the purpose that
we have chosen.

As long as you choose to regard other men and the
events of life solely as they concern your own daily life
and feelings, your mind will be swept hither and thither
by the winds that blow from everywhere.   The mind
will be full of memories and anticipations which habitually suggest emotions of anxiety, regret or resentment.
These suggestions may be for the most part latent when
you are engrossed in some physical work, or some mental activity which is kept to the point by having a physical
basis, such as study or reading from books, or thinking
in the course of conversation with others.   But as soon
as you turn away from active pursuits or study to engage
in concentration especially when no visible image or
form is employed, you feel this persistent press of
thought, which is then very unwelcome.

It is therefore desirable that you should weaken and
destroy these associations, which are so fruitful of mental and emotional agitation, by constantly regarding
other people and things not as appendages to your own
personal life, as providing you with occasions for resentment or self-gratulation, but rather as working out a
destiny of their own, in which you can help them or
hinder them, as you will.   In practice this means that
you should form the habit of considering another man's
actions, motives, words or conduct, not as they affect

your own life and whatever *you* may be interested in, but as they affect his life and interests.

This unselfish mode of life prevents the accumulation of personal thoughts, and certainly concentration cannot be fully accomplished unless it is seriously undertaken. The states of mind during concentration and during the rest of the day react upon each other, and if you can thus to a large extent eliminate anxiety, greed, envy, jealousy, anger, fear, pride and irritability from your daily life, it will be so much the better for your concentration.

ONE-POINTED PURPOSE

If you have already said: "I will," all this will be done, and your concentration will not be disturbed by such thoughts and feelings as these, which constitute the major part of the intruding thoughts that populate the spaces around you. If you have said: "I will," you cannot even wish that certain thoughts should not intrude; if you find yourself wishing this at any time you will know that you have not yet really willed.

Proceed then to sort out the facts of your life. Decide (1) what is your principal purpose in life, (2) what subordinate purposes are necessitated by duty, legitimate enjoyment and amusement, and weakness, or by inclinations which you do not feel strong enough to subdue at present, (3) what things are in your power and to what extent they are so, and what are quite out of your power, (4) how those things that are in your power may be altered to suit your purpose, and how the other things also may be employed when they come your way. The first should be your one aim during the time dedicated to concentration of mind; the second constitutes the major portion of your everyday life; the third should help you to carry out the other two calmly and sanely, so that you will not on the one hand strain at a weight which is beyond your strength, or on the other hand be depressed by obstacles which you are really able either to overcome or to circumvent.

Sit down in the morning and consider what things you are likely to meet with during the day, and of each one ask yourself the questions: "Does it serve my principal purpose? Does it belong to my subordinate purposes? How far is it in my power for alteration or for use? What use can I make of it?" And when the day is done go over the same list again, and ask yourself of each item: "Have I made use of this for my principal purpose or a subordinate one? How far was it in my power? What use did I make of it?"

If you are much troubled by these intruding thoughts, when you are sitting down to begin your daily practice ask yourself the question: "What am I about to do?" And answer point by point: "I am going to do so-and-so. Then I am going to do so-and-so." Then ask: "Why am I about to do so-and-so?" And answer: "For such-and-such a purpose." Secondly think: "What is the business of my everyday life?" Look over it briefly, and then clearly formulate the idea: "I have no concern with it during my period of concentration." Finally think: "What thoughts are likely to disturb me during this period? Mr. Ponsonby spoke ill of me; my son disobeyed me; my father misunderstood me; I lost some money; somebody robbed me; I fear that I shall lose my appointment; I want to have a smoke or a drink or to chew something; I wish it wasn't so hot or so cold; I wonder if I shall gain such-and-such a thing; how can I let my superior officer become aware of my many virtues? I wish my wife or my child were not ailing. Oh, when shall I succeed? I wonder if I am making progress; I wish these flies wouldn't bother me."

Let them all come forward in review. Do not aggravate them by a hasty and angry rebuff, but say to each in turn, quietly: "Good morning, sir, I hope you are well. No doubt your business is very pressing. I shall attend to it seriously and fully during the day, and endeavour to give you the most complete satisfaction; but for the next hour I am otherwise engaged. Good morning." Treated thus politely, the visitors will feel constrained to bow themselves out in silence. They will feel that you have made room for them in ordering your life, and on the small pension of thought that you accord them during the day, they will live peaceably until they die.

The intruding thoughts of this class which come to disturb you during your efforts at concentration are due to your keeping open ends of emotion and thought; if then any such intruder still persists in coming in, pause to give it a moment's consideration.

Say to it: "Come, don't interrupt me now. I will attend to you at five o'clock this afternoon," and keep the appointment, and think it *out*. Consider whether it has to do with a matter which is in your power or not. If it is in your power, decide to do something to settle it. If you have done all that you can, or if it is not in your power to settle the matter, decide finally that it has no concern with you and that you will think of it no more.

TELEPATHIC INTRUDERS

There is another class of intruders, which appear to come telepathically from other minds and from the objects around us. In these days of radio communications there need be no difficulty in believing that thoughts coming from other minds influence ours; that our own habitual thoughts hang about us when we are busily engaged, and discharge themselves upon us in our moments of quiet is a matter of common experience.

In many cases intruders of this second class do not excite particular personal emotions. Words, numbers, pictures, ideas, intelligible or unintelligible, come drifting before the mind; and often they have no connection with the incidents, purposes or emotions that govern our daily lives. They come from the things round about us, and from other persons. If the concentration is active and the mind kept vigorously working, these drifting thoughts will come and go, and though they may be seen floating past, they will not be anchored to the attention. If you find that any such drifting thought becomes insistent and persistent, you will also find that you are taking a personal interest in it, and some impatience, irritation, disappointment or anxiety has arisen. In this case the drifting thought has found a relative sleeping in your mind and has awakened it into activity. It should then be treated as an intruder of the first class. You should become so calm mentally that, while your attention is bent upon one thing, you can merely notice the pictures drifting past without paying any attention to them. Later on, after you gain by practice the required calm and concentration, it will be worth while to examine such pictures in detail; but at the present stage any effort to do so would only divert your attention. The formula at this stage is: "Hello, you there again? All right; stay if you like, go if you like. *I don't care.*"

Remember also that when you are thinking of one thing, or mentally concentrating, there is always a penumbra of other thoughts. Sometimes they swim close enough to the centre to come into focus. Do not try to chase them out. Attend to what you are doing, and they will fade away.

THE EFFECT OF SURROUNDINGS

Although I have said that one should learn to concentrate even in a bus or train—anywhere and on any occasion which does not call for vigilance or response on our part, and when no one is talking to us—so that we may be positive and strong in our policy of life, I do not say that we should ignore the conveniences of quietude and non-interruption in our times of special practice. We must be strong enough to face and overcome difficulties, but need not deliberately make or seek them.

Have you noticed the value of a change of surroundings when you want re-creation or a change in yourself? One man I heard about would sometimes find himself restless in bed; then all he had to do was to put on his clothes and go and lie on the living-room sofa and he would sleep like a top. In concentration also we need not fight the suggestiveness of our surroundings. Some people go to extremes in this, and why not, for everyone should be allowed his whim.

In that case, in order to eliminate both the habitual mental suggestions from familiar objects, and the "crystallized telepathy" of thoughts stamped for a while upon objects which have been in contact with other people, some devices such as the following may be adopted. They may be ignored if your concentration is good, but if at first you do not feel that you can remain entirely unaffected by foreign influences, you may reduce them by the following and similar external devices: Keep for the practice a room which is used for no other purpose. Keep it clean yourself; do not send servants in to handle things. Sit in the middle of the room, and place before you a picture or an image or a symbol (if you have no objection to such forms) of any object or idea you wish to dwell upon. Sit with your back to the window, leaving your ordinary clothes outside. Put on a special garment, preferably not of wool, before going into the room. Do not take into the room money, pocket-knife or keys. Keep a special watch or little clock, pencil and paper there. If it is not too cold, let the feet be bare and well washed before you enter. It is best also to sluice the body and limbs with cold water. All this will keep you from immediate contact with emanations from objects which have been much handled by other people, or used in the business of life, and will also form a wall against drifting thoughts.

But nearly all of this is quite unnecessary, and absolutely so if you have already said: "I will," though at all times and in all cases you will do well to preserve reasonable cleanliness and a considerable amount of silence about what you are doing, so as (1) not to establish in your own mind associations of other people in relation to your practice of concentration, and (2) not to set up telepathic connections related to your concentration and its time and place. Do not start Mr. Smith looking at his watch and saying to Mr. Jones, "Ah, Mr. Robinson will now be doing his concentration in his little garden-pavilion."

CHAPTER VIII

GYMNASTICS OF CONCENTRATION

DIRECT AND INDIRECT THINKING

THE explanations and practices of concentration given up to this point should enable the student to follow a line of thought fairly steadily. Next comes thinking. Thinking is the combining of two or more ideas to embody another idea, which is no more contained in the originals than water is contained in hydrogen and oxygen. In some cases, as in learning, two ideas are given, and to understand the matter we have to think them into a unity. Teachers say that the three angles of a triangle equal two right angles. We have to think how it comes about that that is so. To do this we concentrate on a triangle. Having this very clear in mind, we then think of two right angles side by side. Thinking is thus an extension of the practice of concentration, and depends upon it.

Another occasion of thinking occurs when we use it for discovery. In this case we hold all the data or facts in mind and review them in all their relationships until the new idea pops up. Mons. and Mme. Curie peeped into their laboratory one dark night and saw a glow in some little dishes in which they had evaporated a liquid. "That is not merely dust," they exclaimed. They began to think, "It must be something that we missed in our analysis. What is it?" Somewhat thus radium was discovered.

Concentration is needed for thinking. The stronger the grip and fuller the grasp of the concentration the more direct and less wandering the thinking will be. One person, thinking from A to B may wander about before reaching his goal, as in the following diagram:

while a more trained mind will reach its conclusion almost in a straight line. So let us try a series of experiments calculated to strengthen concentration-on-the-move.

EXERCISES IN SEQUENCE

Exercise 5. Look round a room, noticing the various objects in order. Close the eyes and review them mentally. Again, follow a procession of the letters of the alphabet, and any different alphabets you may know, such as the Greek, Russian, Hebrew, or Devanagari.

Exercise 6. Take a mental walk along a familiar street, remembering whatever details you can. Return by the same route.

Exercise 7. Live over again, in imagination, a part of a day's experience.

Exercise 8. Trace back a series of causes in connection with a familiar object. For example, the clock.

You see the movement of the hands and hear its ticking, and ask what is the cause. You will see the clock on its way from where it was to where it is, back in the factory, the making of its parts, the production of its materials and so on. I introduced into the junior classes in some of the schools in my charge in India a lesson called "The Story of the Shirt" which sometimes went on for about twenty lesson periods, showing the youngsters how, merely putting on a shirt, they were linking up socially with thousands of people, some of whom were in distant parts of the world. It was intended to arouse socially reciprocal feelings, but was also a good training in consecutive thought.

In the above exercises, exact correctness is not essential. Concentration-on-the-move is the aim. You will remember, no doubt, to set up the concentration-mood before you begin.

EXERCISES IN GRASP

Exercise 9. This could be called expansion of concentration. One day I asked a student to imagine a five-pointed star and tell me what he saw. He said that he could not see it all at once, but seemed to have a sort of mental astigmatism, whereby he saw only one or two points clearly, while the others were "out of focus" or even "out of sight" as he described it. I set him to concentrate on one point only until it was clear, then on a second point alone, then on both together, side by side, then to drop this compound and concentrate on still another point, then to recall the compound and add it on, and so on. In this way he succeeded in getting the whole figure clear and in focus. Practise this with several different geometrical figures.

Exercise 10. When the figures mentioned in Exercise 9 are clear, practise a gradual enlargement and reduction of size. You will find that a certain size is best for you for each object. This is true for geometrical figures, and even more obviously so for a natural object. Thinking of an inkstand I will surely find the natural size best, but if my object is a mouse I will do well to magnify it a little, or if it is an elephant to reduce it to, let us say, half the size. This will be evident to anyone who has stood or sat quite near to an elephant for any length of time, as I once did for about two hours. You must either get farther away or else reduce the object.

Exercise 11. Set up in front of you a picture of a human face, or a portrait of someone you like. Look at it carefully and experiment to see how much of it you can imagine clearly at once. Have you omitted the ears? Anyhow, the practice is as follows. Take a small part, such as one eye. Compare your thought with the original. Correct it. Repeat. When the eye is clear and strong, *drop it*, and begin on the other eye. You must drop the first part of the face in order to bring all the power of your mind to bear on the second. In the previous exercises you will have acquired the experience necessary to know that what you have fully concentrated upon will come up very well when recalled, so now you will have faith in this method and confidence in yourself. Next, with the second eye clear, recall the first and think of both together as one picture. Concentrate well on this. Then *drop* the whole and attend to the nose. And so on.

Exercise 12. This exercise deals with a natural scene. I had in my room in India a very attractive picture of Shri Krishna as a boy seated on a boulder in a field and playing the flute. Scattered about the field were several cows happily grazing as far as the bank of a peaceful river. The whole scene was enclosed, as it were, by some tree-clad hills and white clouds in a blue sky.

Imagine the entire scene, then contract your mental picture by gradually dropping the sky and hills, the foreground of grass and small flowers and the portion containing cows and trees on either side, until you have only the boy on the rock. Continue till you have only the spot between the eyes. Then expand the image gradually until you have the whole scene again.

Choose any scene you like, but preferably something agreeable and serene.

EXERCISES IN SELF-EXPANSION

Exercise 13. I am sitting at a table, but I imagine that I am an artist out in a field painting a tree. How nice this picture looks, with two branches on this side and three on that, and what a nice curve of foliage the greenery makes. Yet, somehow, it lacks! And the trunk. It does look a bit like a leg of Uncle Abe's working trousers!

First, then, I am at this side of it, painting those two and three branches and the foliage and the trunk standing on the ground. Then I am at the other side. Then I am up in the air, painting it from above (I had better think, "I am in the sky," else I shall be in a restless aeroplane; we have childhood pictures of God well established in the clouds and peeping through the spaces between, which were quite restfully depicted.) Then I am down in the depths, and the earth has become transparent, and I picture the base of that trunk, which has no base but curvingly loses itself into numerous tails called roots.

Try this practice first with a small object, such as a little statuette on your table. Imagine yourself to be looking down upon it from above. For this purpose transfer your consciousness into the ceiling. Then bring your consciousness down, and go carefully and slowly round the object at a little distance, observing it from every point of view. Next get your consciousness down into the floor and observe the thing from underneath. And finally, by going through all these circumambulations of consciousness one after another with increasing rapidity, try to blend all the images that you have gained from the different points of view, and grasp the thing as it really appears without reference to your position with regard to it.

This is, of course, a difficult thing to do; but remember in these exercises one is not expected to do the thing perfectly, but only to *try*.

Exercise 14. Select now a smallish object which gives a feeling of something enclosed, such as your jewel-box (if any) or a can of peas. There is the can on the table. I put myself into the can. The can is my skin and I am there inside. I become small. I move about among the peas. I look at and admire those tremendous bowls and domes. I become a point in the very centre and from there look at the whole of the inside of the can. I enlarge myself slowly, equating myself to the can and seeing the whole of the inside of it with a "skin-view inlook". I expand myself as big as the room and look at the can from every point of view.

Do this with any chosen object. Repeat the contraction and expansion two or three times at a sitting.

Exercises in Mental Command

Exercise 15. You will by now have discovered that you are able to call up images far more easily than you could before, and that the mind no longer wanders away so wilfully as it used to do. The next step is to make a series of experiments in calling up images bodily and complete before the mind. For this purpose you will probably find that repetition of the name of the object is necessary at first. Suppose that you have been using a portrait in one of the foregoing exercises. Now, with your eyes closed, look into empty space and mentally call out the name of the person depicted, repeating it again and again and trying to discern the form. Suddenly it will spring up before your mental vision, and the complete picture will present itself in idea or in form.

Vary this exercise with the practice of "transformations," somewhat as follows. There is a paper-knife on the table. Shut your eyes and imagine it. Convert it gradually into a pen. Change its form gradually into a statuette of a horse—it has thickened, shortened, curved itself, sprouted legs and tail, modified one end to a head. Modify this into a human statue. Now let it become a pagoda, a tower, a fountain, a tree and so on. Make the transformations as slowly as possible, and try to avoid any abruptness or jerkiness in the thought-stream.

CONCENTRATION AND STUDY

I need make only a few remarks in this book about reading and study.[1]   I advise all people when reading light literature to pause frequently to remind themselves to make clear mental pictures of what they read.   Our hero comes to the house to call for his girl friend to take her to a dance.   We must seem to see his car edge in to the curb, and the hero getting out, crossing the pavement, mounting the steps, ringing the bell, removing his hat, arriving within, and then we behold him becoming suitably reserved and abashed in the presence of the wonderful young maiden standing there, who now etc. etc. . . . If it is worth reading it is worth seeing, and also thinking about.

In the case of serious study, do not forget to concentrate on one idea at a time.   Say to yourself after the first swift reading of a paragraph: "There are four ideas here.   I must use concentration on each one of them separately, and then combine them into a larger mental picture, as I did when concentrating on a portrait." Each new idea will become clear to you when you concentrate fully upon it, thinking of other things in comparison with it, noticing all the resemblances, differences and relationships you can.

---

[1] For full treatment of this subject see *Mind and Memory Training* by Ernest Wood. Pub. by Sir Isaac Pitman and Sons, Ltd. , London, England.

CHAPTER IX

WHAT MEDITATION IS

CONCENTRATION AND MEDITATION

WHEN the student is well practised in concentration, so that he can put on the mood of it like a garment, let him or her proceed to meditation and contemplation.

In all our acting and thinking we shuttle to and fro between two poles of our being—advancing without and retreating within, in both of which we become more and more alive, until we are sufficiently mature to unite the two.

Advancing without. I may look at a flower casually as I pass. I have not been properly aware of its qualities, but only that there is a flower there. But I could pause attentively, and say:

"That yellow colour is really nice. How yellow it is! And the shape is beautiful, as the petal turns this way, then that way! And the scent is delicious! And the texture—it is heavenly!"

When I thus pause I bring more of myself to the flower. In this moment I am wedded to the flower. We live together, without reservations. I give myself to the flower, and I believe that in some unseen way the life in the flower is also enhanced. At all events I am enhanced, to a point of great happiness. Let me enjoy this moment of rich living. Let me not lose any of it, even by thinking, "What can I do to preserve this moment?" I need not fear to give myself, for I cannot give myself away.

In thus bringing more of myself to the flower, I am more awake and alive than I was.

But there is death—the moment dies, the pause dies, the flower dies.

Retreating within. Still, I do not die. In a quiet place in my house, and in a quieter place in my mind and heart, the moment lives for ever. I recall it. "A pale simulacrum of the moment," someone may say. Not so. Pale simulacra result from pale living. Anyhow, now pause, eyes closed, and take the memory of that flower within, into the depths of your thought. Say to yourself, "Here I am, a mind. Alas, a flat, dull and seemingly unprofitable mind." Perhaps; but not so, if you say, "Come in, little flower, into my lonely mind." And you meditate with the flower. And soon you will be worshipping the flower and saying, "Wonderful flower, holy flower—forgive me, forgive me, my pride and contumely." And the flower will forgive, and there will be love and ecstasy. That is meditation.

Our life is the same at both poles. By bringing out the whole of myself to meet the world my life is enhanced. By taking that realest experience within, it is still further enhanced. And just as the outer experience gives a vividness to be carried into the meditation, so does the meditation give new power to future experience. After the meditation I may meet the flower again, and it will be to me more a flower than it was before—in colour, form, scent and everything.

How I am made strong by this shuttle action of full living!

It is a shuttle action that will produce full cloth, for soon my meditation-mood will be present while I am advancing without and the object-experience will be clear and strong when I am retreating within.

The whole of life is of this kind and follows this process, but ordinarily it is carried on without much attention. The world seems designed for this purpose. We make things—and in so doing concentrate upon them; and then they react upon us. As we go through life, it is as though we were children making toys for ourselves, playing with them awhile, and then turning to something else. The toy is a limitation to the child, inasmuch as it engrosses the attention in the small field of the object and out of the wider and more diffuse field of indefinite attention. Even the body and the senses conduce to the same end, shutting out most of the world and admitting only a little of it, but that little is clear and strong, somewhat as in a camera a distant picture is formed upon the plate or film because the small hole in front admits only a limited quantity of light rays. I have often thought that if ordinary men could suddenly be endowed with super-physical senses, as they sometimes wish, they would not benefit thereby, but would be overwhelmed by the variety and volume of new experience. There would not be enrichment of mind, but only worse confusion than already is, as if in the round of daily action we were to see all the operations of the interior of the body. The consciousness of the average man is sufficiently diffused and indefinite; let him practise concentration so as to make it clearer and stronger, and then meditation so as to expand that clearer, stronger, consciousness over a larger field. Let him become master of himself in the small region where he is ruler, and then the time will be ripe for him to have a more expanded life.

Returning to meditation, notice that it is preceded always by concentration, that concentration produces a very wide-awake consciousness, consciousness at its best, and that in meditation this wide-awakeness is preserved and applied to full reflection upon a chosen subject. Meditation is thus the opposite of going to sleep. It is the very completion of thought upon that subject. Sleep, mind-wandering, day-dreaming, drift, dullness and disorder are all absent in meditation.[1]

As, in a sense, all healing is self-healing, or from within, and the doctor can only prescribe the conditions in which that can be least obstructed, or, in a garden the gardener can only provide the soil, water, sunshine and protection needed by the plant for its growth from within, so it seems there is some higher life within us waiting to bring us to superior conscious living. Sometimes people think of such a life as above us, rather than within. This is not so intimate, but may do us no harm and produce no obstructive thought if we remember that it

---

[1] Patanjali, the ancient exponent of meditation, whose aphorisms are acknowledged to this day all over India to be the most informative ever written on the subject, gave the whole process as threefold—concentration, followed by meditation, passing on to contemplation. His definitions of concentration and meditation are (1) Concentration is the binding of the mind to one place, and (2) Meditation is continued mental effort there. This is my own translation, which is very literal. For a full treatment of all the 194 aphorisms, see my *Practical Yoga: Ancient and Modern.* (Pub. by Rider & Co., London, and E. P. Dutton & Co., New York.)

is only a simile—a mental idol.   On these lines one may
consider the following diagram:

The first jar represents the ordinary man; the three
levels of the jar, the physical, emotional and mental sec-
tions of his personal constitution. Physically he is
restless and distracted by everything that touches his
senses; emotionally he has little self-control, and the
most trifling event can destroy his balance for a considerable time: mentally, his life is almost without direction
at all.   The water pouring down from above represents
the life within, which is dissipated through the innumerable holes in the vessel.

The second figure shows the man of meditation. By
concentration he closes up the holes, and the water,
pouring into him in ever-increasing volume, fills up the
vessel constantly higher and higher; and the life within

does creative work up to the level which it has reached. Do not, therefore, think of meditation as something to soothe you when in trouble, or as a means of escape from the world, but think of it as the way to rise to a higher platform of consciousness, so that, facing the world with that new consciousness, you will attain greater reality, and so proceed in a "virtuous circle" to the realization of an altogether fuller and richer life and consciousness. In common life, remember, one person's consciousness is a poor, dull thing, merely a flickering candle, while that of another is a strong and steady glow, taking its power from some universal electric fount; secondly, that the difference between these two is one of education through experience; thirdly, that we have reached a point where education can be quickly fulfilled by self-education through voluntary experience; and fourthly that we know not the heights of attainment except that from the words of Buddhas and Christs we know that there is something there. Perhaps even now some of us see as in a glass darkly what we shall afterwards—when we will have it so—see openly and face to face.

MEDITATION AND EXPERIENCE

I hope it has become clear that meditation is no retreat from the world but is one pole of our terrestrial conscious activity which is all creative. Not by meditation alone will anyone reach to the greatest heights; the limitations of external life contain the divine teaching in equal measure. To look within and to seek without are the winter and the summer, the day and the night, the left and the right foot of the soul's progress. Just as one who understands may be as thrilled with the beauty of a tiny leaf as with the grandeur of a tropical forest, so may one know that the divine finger is just as much in the small experience that comes to you and me as it is in the great occurrences which make landmarks in history. Our life sways between the inner and the outer poles. Inward thought devises a machine or propounds a theory; outward experience suggests improvements to that mechanism, or declares the theory true or false. Consistency with the laws of nature, in their multifarious interplay, alone makes a thing useful or proves a theory true. As it was said that there is no bar or wall in the human soul where God the cause leaves off and man the effect begins, so it may be said that there is no point or place in the world of experience where these two do not meet.

Meditation, therefore, is most effectual when its thoughts and emotions are carried out of the chamber into the affairs of life, there to receive correction and modification, there to have attached to them points of experience that will give them new bloom and add to them sister blossoms in future meditations.

MEDITATION AND HUMAN EVOLUTION

The following diagram is intended to give a rough idea of the changes which occur in man in the course of his development. The first figure indicates the condition of an undeveloped man, in whom the physical nature is dominant and the will is weak, the second that of one very advanced in whom the balance is reversed; other people lie between the two.

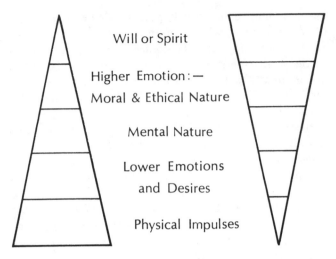

Will or Spirit

Higher Emotion:—
Moral & Ethical Nature

Mental Nature

Lower Emotions
and Desires

Physical Impulses

The diagram also indicates what I explained before. In early stages of human growth desires are few. The savage accepts the comforts that nature gives, and only occasionally stirs his body into great activity for the satisfaction of desires. He is ruled by the immediate surroundings of his body. But a little later we find that life has become more complex; the desire-nature has considerably awakened, and, seeking to gratify desire more and more, men have multiplied life's activities to a great extent. It is the man's desire that is now the strongest thing in him—immediate physical ease must take second place. Desire causes him to select one of the many lines of action that are possible at a given moment. At this stage the mind, so far as it is developed, works only as a servant of desire, planning for its fulfilment in action.

But in the course of development the mind grows until it becomes the higher authority and begins to select among desires. Desires and emotions multiply to such an extent that a conflict arises among them, as they cannot all be satisfied at once. Then each prefers its claim before the intellect, and by thought a man begins to select the desires that are desirable and separate them from the desires that are undesirable, and to say to himself: "I will allow myself to desire this, not that." Thus the man learns to follow law.

We may carry the argument a step further, and declare that when the processes of the thinking mind are controlled by the ethical nature a man will begin to value life-contacts more than thing-contacts. Next he begins to discover the spiritual will that lies behind, between and above even the ethical life, and to know what it is he is doing and has to do. This attainment means that the man is conscious that he is something above mind and thought, even while mental activity is going on, just as a cultured man may recognize that he is something above and beyond his body, even while he is walking down the street.

Let us distinguish clearly between modes of knowing and knowledge itself. Language is a mode of knowing. When we have formulated facts in satisfactory words it is our habit to believe that we then know those facts. But words are only a lower vehicle of knowledge, a substitute for facts, like the terms in algebra; at best they only suggest ideas, they cannot replace them and they must be transcended as we approach closer to a real knowledge of the relations between things. All the forms that we see and that we can visualise are only an imperfect mode of knowledge, and they also will be transcended in due course. This does not mean, however, that intuitional knowledge is less definite than what is embodied in words; though it might seem so to one who approaches it by metaphysical argument, it certainly does not appear so to one who reaches it directly by the practice of meditation.

It is not difficult to give reasons why the lower mind must sooner or later yield its place of authority in human life to a higher intuition. Here are several:

(1) Carefully analyse the analytical faculty of mind. How do we observe things? By comparison; by noting points of similarity and of difference. But to distinguish one thing perfectly its comparison with all others is required; and as this is true of all things perfect perception sees them all to whatever it turns, and discrimination of the many things as different thus disappears. Analysis is analysed away.

(2) Again, in the current of events one thing is what and where and when it is because all things are so; and since this is true of all things, particular causality disappears. We are indeed whirling through space, mentally as well as physically, on a ball which has itself no foundation or support.

(3) The conception of the object of contemplation as something outside of me, which I am observing, is absurd. There is no line where "I" leaves off and "that" begins. The distinction between the subject and the object vanishes when we realise that these are only two ends of one stick, or that the "I" is the unchanging, unmodified witness of all the changes and modifications within itself.

There *is* another state of existence, or rather another form of life, beyond the mind, with its laboured process of discernment of comparisons and causal relations between things. That higher state is only to be realised when the activities of consciousness are carried, in all their earthly fervor and vigour, beyond the groping cave-life in which they normally dwell. That higher consciousness will come to all men sooner or later; and when it comes to any one of us all his life will suddenly appear changed. We shall no longer be staggered by the thought of eternal life in an ever-changing universe of time; we shall not now be appalled by the fearful possibility of eternal rest in changelessness; for these are but the conceptions of the little mind, applying its puny standards to the limitless glory of the life divine.

CHAPTER X

METHODS OF MEDITATION

PRELIMINARY PRACTICES

MEDITATION is a complete flow of thought about an object which you have successfully concentrated upon. It is not a flow past, like a procession in the street, but a flow into, a filling-up. It is like a thread of thoughts closely wound into a ball, such that every part of the thread is intimate with every other part. In meditation you enfold yourself in a cocoon of your thoughts; you go in a grub and come out a butterfly.

There are certain preliminary practices which are a great aid to meditation. First, there is the simple method of sparing a little time each morning or evening to turning over in the mind the events of the day, and thinking about them in a gentle manner. This is a great rest and recreation for mind, emotions and body; it purifies and refines our lives and ploughs and harrows the field, preparing it for inspiration and intuition.

Secondly, the manner of our reading can also provide good preparation for meditation. Let it not be too casual—except in those times when we intentionally read merely for relaxation—but let us pay careful attention to the scene, that the characters may walk and talk like real beings before our eyes. Best of all, let us think before and after. We shall gain much more from our novel or story if we (1) reflect upon the portion previously read and the situation reached, (2) read, and then (3) reflect upon that which we have now read. In the reflection it is necessary only to pass the material in review; thinking upon it will arise spontaneously.

If it is study we are doing, the value of such reflection is inestimable. If I am going to read about geraniums, let me first ask myself what I already know about geraniums, and not be satisfied with a superficial answer, but try to name all the facts I can—geraniums I have seen and read about, varieties of geraniums, the parts and qualities of geraniums, the effect of geraniums upon things and people. This practice will revive and co-ordinate the ideas already in my mind, and it will also awaken in it many questions. Now I shall bring to the reading an orderly mind, active in relation to the subject, and also alert to pick up items of information where it has become conscious of a lack. After reading, let me again reflect, asking myself what new knowledge I have gained, and perhaps causing myself to turn back to the book to see whether it really said so-and-so, or what it said on such-and-such a point, about which I am uncertain. These reflections clear up disorder in the mind, and at the same time help to remove the other two d's of the mind—dullness and drift.

Meditation is used by different people for different purposes. I need not comment on the respective merits of their aims; my business is to describe the various methods which can help each one in his chosen line, and to mention any dangers by the way.

MEDITATION ON OBJECTS

What have I here? A pebble from a beach in Cyprus, now used as a paperweight. Let me meditate on this. First I shall observe it very carefully, noting its size, shape, colour, texture, heaviness, markings, etc. Next, I shall close my eyes and concentrate upon it. Now I will use the Four Roads of Thought again, with a new motive—to realize as fully as possible the object in whole and parts, its qualities and its actions. When I have done my best at this I shall know that pebble better than before—both it and its relation to other things. The fullness of meditation on the form and colour of this object will lead to a realization of beauty more than I knew before. If this does not come from the whole, it will come from meditation on a part of it.[1] Meditation on its substance and weight and stillness will lead to a new realization of what be-ing is. Another line of meditation will lead me to feel what it would be like to have one's consciousness in the stone. I must merge myself in it and feel the "stoneness" of it. What is that life experiencing? What "stillness" is it feeling, learning and enjoying?

If my object was a living thing—the cat, again—I should have much more scope for meditation. After

---

[1] Perfect meditation will be on the whole thing, but if in the course of a meditation we feel we want to continue it only on a part, we can reduce the field of concentration to that part, whereupon that part becomes the object of meditation. Thus, if I am meditating on an elephant, and I find I become especially interested in its strength only, I can reduce the field from elephant (which now becomes a background) to the aspects or examples of strength which it presents.

following all the Roads, I would come to the question of the feelings of the cat in many different situations. And again, I would merge myself in the cat mind, and bathe, as it were, in its consciousness and experience. Already I have tasted its sensitiveness, its beauty, and its being in poise and in motion, and now, entering its consciousness I shall know it by the road of love, a feeling of its feelings which I cannot have without being attentive to its outlook. In order to learn skill in action, how to touch things, how to walk with touch and balance, and many other such things, I will do well to meditate upon the cat. Every animal has something very valuable for us.

In both cases—the stone and the animal—my thought, feelings and body will all be improved by meditation.

PRACTICAL EXERCISES

Exercise 16. Consider again the diagram and arrow-words on page 17. Recall how you made a larger diagram or chart for yourself, with perhaps fifty or more arrow-words about the cat or other chosen object. In that practice of concentration, every time that you thought of something directly (not meditatively) concerned with the cat you wrote it down as an arrow-word. You did not then allow yourself to think *about* this arrow-word, but dropped it from mind and slid back along the arrow to the central thought, the cat.

Now get out your old sheet of paper containing your diagram with all its arrow-words, or make a new one. Do not be in a hurry; it will not be a waste of time to make a new one, if necessary. Using this diagram or chart, look at arrow-word number 1, which may be "milk" (for example), and return (sliding, not jumping) to the cat, *bringing the milk with you.* Now you will spend a little time looking at the cat and the milk *together* as a unitary mental picture, thinking all you can about their relationship, when this flow of thought (in which you do not allow yourself to think about milk except with the intention of its relation to the cat—for that would be starting a new chart with milk in the centre) is finished, and you feel that nothing more is coming up in mind on the subject of this relationship, you turn to your arrow-word number 2 and treat it in the same way, and so on with all your arrow-words.

This is meditation on the cat, and as a result of it you will have enormously enriched your idea (and future experience) of cats, and will have co-ordinated many disorderly and disconnected pieces of knowledge lying scattered about in your mind, and you will have increased your power and ease of thinking, so that in future your fountain of thought *on any subject* will play more readily and fully than before. You will probably also have received some new thoughts coming intuitively, as it were, for in all thinking there is a little touch (or more) of your original power, of which every consciousness has a share. But it must be said that this intuition belongs to the contemplation (into which one may slip involuntarily now and then during the practice) rather than to the thinking or meditation.

Practise this method with several material objects, and with living objects—such as animals. Practise first with paper and diagram, and afterwards in the mind only without a chart, according to desire.

Meditation on Virtues

Exercise 17. The way to meditate on a virtue is simple. First of all make concrete pictures of the virtue in action. For each virtue make a number of pictures; compare them and try to find what is the essential of the virtue and what is the feeling of the virtue in action. Do not be satisfied with mere pictures, as though they were being played before you on a stage. Step up on to the stage and merge yourself in the action, thinking and feeling at the same time. Thirdly, go beyond this, and find yourself to be the internal spectator of the virtue, in which condition you witness it as in the "you," not in the "I," of yourself. Fourthly, return to your meditation on the virtue as such, but seeing how it would apply in many different circumstances, and in each case putting yourself into the scene and action.

Should one practise meditation for the removal of faults? It is not good to meditate on faults. Faults are to die, not to be killed. They arise from unbalance of virtues. If you must dwell on your faults, observe that they arise from the lack of some virtue, and meditate upon that. Our ideal life is active, loving and thoughtful—all three together—and the corresponding faults are laziness, selfishness and thoughtlessness. When something goes wrong, find out which of these faults has spoiled the work of the other two virtues, and then meditate upon its opposite virtue; all faults are due to deficiencies. There is no evil in any man.

In writing on meditation on virtues I wish to safeguard the student on the point. It is not our aim to form a habit of thinking about ourselves as virtuous, but to establish the virtues in our minds and hearts so as to forget them when they have sunk into the subconscious, and become spontaneous or reflex. It is quite analogous to that attention to the body which gives it, through suitable exercises, balanced musculature and good ways of breathing, eating, sleeping, talking, standing, sitting and walking. In both body and mind these functions (habits of the body, and virtues of the mind) are intended to permit the work of life to go on well. This is the real meditation—that work-meditation which makes us receive and attend to the world in a proper spirit and manner and carry on our own work with the skill and perfection that a good body and mind must inevitably achieve. Do we not all value this kind of life and work, which automatically and unconsciously presents and produces harmony and beauty, and do we not instinctively avoid and dislike (1) livelihoods which are characterized by cunning planning to obtain the fruit of others' work, and (2) living to be good, which is merely self-gratulation and is not true living? If we find these two faults in our lives, let us with all speed flee them by full attention to the work of living, which lies in the true meeting of what is without and what is within, wherein both the world and the man are spontaneously improved. Virtues are really attained only when they have gone into the subconscious.

MEDITATION ON THE LAWS

It is worth while to spare a little time to meditate quietly upon material and spiritual laws. There is, for example, the law of gravity. Knowing it, we should be fools indeed to jump downstairs instead of walking, or to attempt to cross a river on our feet. There are the laws of health, governing sleep and work and food and many other things, and here again we know that disobedience is foolishness, ruinous to health and happiness

As there are laws for the body, so are there spiritual laws for the soul, of which the voice of conscience occasionally reminds us. Those spiritual laws are interested in the whole of our life's journey, not only the bit of it that we now know. Yet they are in no wise contrary to material ones, because at last our physical life has a spiritual basis. Honesty and truth-speaking, for example, build up social relations that rest upon our confidence in one another and lead to co-operation and prosperity.

Meditation on the spiritual laws can polarize all our thoughts and emotions into line with them, and make our most common daily contacts with others a spiritual voyage instead of a material battle. To live—not shrink from life, but bring to it all we are and all we have—with love and thought—is the fundamental spiritual law for us. It is three in one at all times, any one of which we ignore at our peril. Some may say: "I will work now, get money, and love my friends at the card party this evening." But the carpenter who makes a chair, considering the comfort, durability and beauty of it, and happy in the thought that someone will find it satisfactory and will really enjoy it, is fulfilling the spiritual law.

DEVOTIONAL MEDITATION

Many people who are devotional by nature prefer to meditate on the ideal human being, instead of on the

virtues.   Sometimes they choose for this (1) a real his-
torical person and sometimes (2) a symbolic figure.
Thought here is two-fold—one group finds delight in
self-abandonment or adoration, the other in service of
the ideal person.   The latter, however, is like the former
for purposes of meditation, for without the knowledge
and nearness that meditation brings one is not likely to
perform true service, that is, act with intelligent love.

In this group comes the worship of "idols" or pictures
and images.   Certain Hindu schools of thought recommend their devotees to use these if necessary in order to
obtain strong thoughts, but always remembering that
there is no such real being.   The benefit is somewhat of
the nature of that obtained by a little girl playing very
seriously with a doll—the child never completely forgets
that this is not a real baby, yet the make-believe helps
her to unfold her latent emotions.

At the back of all devotional meditation is the idea
that men come to resemble what they dwell upon in
their thought.   Because of this we need that meditation
which will take our thought to the very depths of the
object of devotion, the mind behind the face, and the
god behind the mind.

Knowing the value of this method, the Hindus have
long lists of qualities, enumerating the virtues of the
divine being.   There is some danger, however, when
so many forms are taken, of repeating mere words, without realizing and feeling the effect of each one as fully
as possible.   Mere repetition of vaguely understood
words and phrases would only produce a kind of mental
and moral hypnotism.   Ponder upon the quality as
manifest in the form that is selected for meditation, and

take the quality in all its aspects and relationships.   At the outset a set of questions may be used to stimulate the thought, but when that is made clear, pondering and dwelling upon it, and viewing it in different lights are necessary.   Such questions are: Why does the divine one possess and show this quality?   How?   To whom?   When?   In what degree?   In what manner?   With what effect?   A list of qualities can easily be extracted from any book of divine praise of any religion.

I find the preparation for this process so beautifully drawn in an old Sanskrit book that I cannot refrain from offering a translation of the passage.   By such a process of imagination a devotee may withdraw himself from the depressing suggestions of a dingy room, wrapping himself first in a scene of beauty and peace, and then enjoying therein quiet meditation upon a beloved form.

"Let him find in his heart a broad ocean of nectar.
　Within it a beautiful island of gems,
Where the sands are bright golden and sprinkled
　　with jewels.
　Fair trees line its shores with a myriad of blooms,
And within it rare bushes, trees, creepers and rushes,
　On all sides shed fragrance most sweet to the sense.

"Who would taste of the sweetness of divine com-
　　pleteness
　Should picture therein a most wonderful tree,
On whose far-spreading branches grow fruit of all
　　fancies—
　The four mighty teachings that hold up the world.

There the fruit and the flowers know no death and
  no sorrows,
  While to them the bees hum and soft cuckoos sing.

"Now, under the shadow of that peaceful arbour,
  A temple of rubies most radiant is seen.
And he who shall seek there will find on a seat rare,
  His dearly Beloved enshrined therein.
Let him dwell with his mind, as his teacher defines,
  On that Divine Form, with its modes and its
  signs."

A Christian would generally select as his personal
object the Christ amid the scenes of the gospel stories.
The Hindus have a great variety of forms and incarnations of Shiva and Vishnu, and of Parvati, Lakshmi and
Saraswati. Among them it is customary to use many
symbols in these meditations. For example, in a certain meditation connected with the throat centre, the
yogis think of the great Sadasiva; he is of a snow-white
colour; is clothed in a tiger's skin; has five faces with
three eyes each, and has ten arms, each of which bears
a symbol of power or exhibits a certain sign—a trident,
a battle-axe, a sword, a thunderbolt, a snake, a bell, a
goad, a noose, and a gesture of dispelling fear. This
is only one of dozens of such symbolic forms. I will
give an account of one such form of meditation in
chapter XI.

Exercise 18. Select your ideal, the object of your
worship, and take care when you do so that there is
nothing in it that you in any way dislike or fear. Let
it be one which you can fully trust and never question

at all, for to besmirch the mind with a deity who needs glossing over, polishing or veneering, is to prostitute the loftiest human faculty, the power of worship, to the base uses of worldly hopes and fears.

When you have decided upon a suitable object, make an image of it before your mind, fix your attention upon it, and allow your thought to play upon it with an uninterrupted flow, so that as you dwell upon it from different aspects it constantly awakens your unselfish emotions.

A safeguard necessary in devotional meditation is that of avoiding self-abasement, due to the thoughts of the gulf between oneself and the object of devotion. In both Christian and Hindu religions the divine Incarnations are held to have the purpose of bringing their votaries up to their own level and into a mystic union of some kind. In view of this, "feeling the gap" is not true reverence, which is a glad acceptance of the divine gift of union, beginning in likeness, which is adoration (which is spiritual "conversation") and passing on into the unity of one spiritual being. "It cannot be expected of people like us . . ." is not a good thought, for in these adorations that "us" will be transformed. The error here mentioned not only reduces the character-building effect; it also leads to harmful judgment of other people, for they, too, are then regarded as mere ordinary people, in whom as such we cannot easily see or admit the virtues predicated of our beloved ideal.

A second safeguard is to remember that the form of the beloved is not really the beloved. The meditation must go inwards—first on the form, then on the emotions, then on the outlook, then on the love, then on the deep purpose, so that the devotee may become one with the beloved in mind and heart and beyond, meeting within, not merely in external form.

A third error often made is that of living in another to compensate your own failure or sense of inferiority, and thus reconciling to yourself your lack of achievement, with a feeling of relief. This is another of the ways in which devotion can stumble and refute its own purpose of assimilating or rising to the divine.

It is not easy to describe devotion; we feel it, but should never let it be a substitute for life nor an enemy of thought and understanding.

MEDITATION ON SENTENCES

To work through a religious or philosophical book and meditate on the sentences is another frequent practice. It supplements (a) reading and (b) study, on the assumption that the writer is expressing deep thought worthy of the profoundest consideration. For example, in an old book I read: "Verily, in whom unwisdom is destroyed by the wisdom of the Self, in them the wisdom, shining as the sun, reveals the Supreme." Every word has to be pondered on to find its full meaning and implication. You have to take the sentence to pieces—to the smallest pieces—and put it together again, knowing that the whole is always more than the sum of its parts. It may require a long time, but you must not be impatient. You must not go on to the next verse or passage as long as you can do anything more with the present one, even if it lasts you for days or weeks. You may have to break the whole sentence again and again, to go back to a part and concentrate and meditate on that, and once more build the whole. Your attention will slide along the sentence, illuminating the parts one after another backwards as well as forwards, until the one fact denoted by the whole is a simple unity, fully present with all its variety of parts, qualities and actions.

In meditation on a sentence or a part of it you must not simply say, "Oh, that's easy, very understandable," and leave it at that, just as you do not say, "That's merely a flower," and pass on. Take the following: "Thy Self is in itself without a body." In the non-casualness of meditation you are to move into a realization of this, or else the teacher has spoken in vain.

Remember that obviousness is often due to casualness, and that you may be walking over a gold-mine without knowing it. The unobvious sometimes reveals its secrets more easily because it puzzles, and thereby commands attention, as in the following passage from Jacob Boehme: "The unground is an eternal nothing, but makes an eternal beginning as a craving. For the nothing is a craving after something. But as there is nothing that can give anything, accordingly the craving itself is the giving of it, which yet also is a nothing, or merely a desirous seeking. And that is the eternal origin of Magic, which makes within itself, where there is nothing, something out of nothing, and that is itself only, though this craving is also a nothing that is merely a will. It has nothing and there is nothing that can give anything; neither has it any place where it can find or repose itself. The craving is certainly a cause of the will, but without knowledge or understanding of the craving.

We recognize, therefore, the eternal will-spirit as God, and the moving life of the craving as Nature."

Exercise 19. Take a short sentence and meditate upon it in the manner described above.

MEDITATION FOR WRITING AND SPEAKING

It is to be assumed that the reader of these lines will not wish to write articles, give lectures or make speeches on any object of which he has not made a conscientious study, for any other course would be definitely unethical, and could be observed to be motived by pride, profit or propaganda. But even when one knows a subject well, there is still the need to see the *whole map* of it, so that one may not over-emphasize any aspect of the subject, on the one hand, or overlook any aspect of it, on the other. Therefore, before writing or speaking, a preliminary systematic review of the subject, which is a kind of meditation, may be undertaken, as follows:

Sit quietly, and tell yourself what the subject you have chosen is. Perhaps you are going to write on "Carbon —its Forms, Attributes and Actions," on "Castles in Spain," on "Falstaff," on "Money—what is it?" or on "The Palingenesis of the Plastidule". Well, then, place the subject in the centre of your attention, then say, "Road 1; Review of Experiences". When these reviews are finished, you proceed to "Road 2; class relationships; resemblances and differences". Next, "Road 3; parts". Next, "Road 4; qualities". In this way your work is not likely to be lop-sided, you are not liable to miss anything of importance, and, what is more, you are likely to have some good ideas, which you may jot down as you go along, which you would have missed if you have simply plunged into your writing without this preliminary meditation.

INTELLECTUAL MEDITATION

In the intellectual form of meditation our purpose is to understand the chosen object as fully as possible. When this is done there is expansion without loss of strength or clarity. When a student is trying to grasp an idea, if he is wise he will first of all concentrate for a while on the data before him, will review his knowledge of them, will study all the things, with their parts, qualities and actions, which bear upon the idea. Then he will put them together, and the new idea will be born in that body of thought or combination he has made. If, however, he finds that he cannot remember all his data at once, that he is constantly losing his facts and has to make an effort to collect them again, he may also note that it is next to impossible to "get the idea" or solve his problem, and that if he does so it occurs more by accident than as the result of his successful work.

In that case he is trying to go too far without sufficient groundwork, and he should go back to the study of his facts, which were themselves built or born from simpler facts a little while ago.

But if, on the other hand, he finds himself able to work his way steadily to his solution, he will probably also find that his data have become additionally clear as well. Expansion has not destroyed clarity in that case. It may be said that in all studies involving any grasp or depth of thought the aim of the student should be to make his conclusion as clear and real and familiar as his premises, so that he may later on use that conclusion as a simple and self-evident datum for his further or deeper investigation.   All the time the student is engaged in making platforms for himself and then climbing on to them.

All thinking is really abstract thinking.   It is one abstract idea that holds two or more concrete ones together.   No one can really think of two quite separate things at once; if it appears to be so, they are parts of one bigger thought.   You can think of one abstract or complex idea which contains two or more others.   Thus, for example, to picture a pen and a hand separately would be difficult, but to picture a pen in the hand in the act of writing is very easy.   That is because that has become one idea for us in the course of our experience.   So the student should never try to grasp a variety of things at once; he will only distress himself and produce a kind of mental panic if he tries to do so.   Let him always look for the abstract connecting ideas, which are really enveloping ideas.

Now we will take some more difficult practices which are bound to seem very unsatisfactory and almost impossible of accomplishment.   They may nevertheless be expected to produce the faculty of inspiration—a deeper working of the higher part of the mind, which flows into action unexpectedly.   It has often been noticed with regard to great scientific discoveries and inventions as well as profound philosophic and religious thoughts that they are due more to inspiration than to logical thinking.   They are seldom the immediate result of a deliberate chain of thought, and yet without that thought they would not have come. It is usually only when the lower mind has tried its best that the higher mind will help. Quite often an inventor or a scientist has puzzled over a problem for a long time and found no solution for it, until suddenly, perhaps some time after he has set it aside as insoluble, the truth has flashed into his mind, illuminating the whole field of enquiry. That is inspiration. It is of the higher mind while intuition proper touches the inner heart and tells of right and wrong, and conscience comes from the inner will.

Exercise 20. Select a difficult or abstract subject, such as the idea of harmony or beauty. Fix your thought upon it. Begin by asking questions about it. What is the selected idea? Name it. Think of some concrete examples of it, such as harmony in music and the harmonic motion of pendulums. See to what senses these examples apply. Go over them in detail and observe their qualities for sensation. What is the class of the idea? What are its prominent features? In what does it resemble and in what does it differ from other similar or contrasting ideas? What is its real nature and why does it exist? What part does it play in the succession of events? From what does it rise and to what does it lead?

When you have to some extent answered all these questions, picture several concrete images together, trying to grasp their common element of harmony. Then try to hold this abstract thought of harmony, while you drop the concrete images.

Exercise 21. Think of a number of colours: red, yellow, green, blue and violet. Notice that these are all distinct and quite different sensations. What do you see? You see red, yellow, green, blue and violet. But you do not see colour, as such. Fix upon two colours, say red and green. Concentrate upon them. What have they in common? Certainly not much as regards their superficial appearance. There is, however, a relation between them, something which is common to them both. It is colour. Try to understand what colour is. Drop the images and thought of red and green, and try to keep hold of the conception of colour without them. Next fix the thought upon heat and cold. We are sensible of different degrees of warmth or coldness, but we have no direct sensation of heat as such. Try, out of these two ideas, to conceive of heat as such. Cling to the conception that you thus obtain while you drop the ideas of different degrees of heat. Again, colour and heat are two forms of sensation. What is it that these have in common? The idea of sensation. Try to grasp this while you drop the ideas of colour and heat. In this practice it is not enough to define the things logically in words by their generic and differentiating marks. They must be pondered upon and looked into with a kind of mental feeling, and then an effort must be made to grasp and hold the abstract idea without any sense of form or of naming.

Exercise 22. Now take up for further practice a series of difficult questions, such as: What is Truth? What is Spirit? What is Justice? Avoid giving mere verbal definitions, but try to realize these things mentally. Follow reason in trying to elucidate them, and when you can reason no further, still do not let the thought wander away. Keep the thought there, at the highest point that you have been able to reach, and wait for the inspiration that will surely come.

MEDITATION WITH MANTRAS

THE NATURE OF MANTRAS

In this chapter I must allow myself to use certain Sanskrit words which have technical importance in the study of the mind and the world. *Mantra* is one of them. In connection with meditation it refers to words or sentences which are repeated over and over again while the mind is intent upon their meaning. I have recently read in one Upanishad the recommendation that a certain 16-syllabled *mantra* should be repeated thirty-five million times, and one commentator offers the calculation that it can be done in twenty years at the rate of about five thousand times each day, or eight times per minute for ten hours!

Without going to such extremes, it is usual for nearly all people who practise meditation in India to perform these recitations, even though only a few times. The ideas are: (1) the words help to keep the mind on the object they refer to, and (2) their repetition or rhythm has an effect on the body. This effect can be understood by reference to the three "qualities of Nature," called *gunas*, which are *tamas*, *rajas* and *sattwa*. These are basic ingredients of material substance, and appear in different proportions in all things. Material, inert, resistant and lazy things and people are called tamasic; the forceful, energetic, excitable, passionate and pushful are called rajasic; and the orderly, rhythmical, constancy-showing, law-abiding are called sattwic. For success in meditation it is desirable that the body should be calm and orderly in all its functions. This we have already considered in early chapters; we have emphasized the importance of using intelligence and will to put and keep the body in this sattwic condition.

The repetition of a *mantra* in meditation is intended to have the double effect of counteracting the sleepiness of *tamas* and the excitability of *rajas*, and establishing *sattwa*. It is not unlike the effect of suitable kinds of music. At the same time I must say that *mantras* are unnecessary, and must in fact be given up before a high state of meditation can be reached or contemplation approached.

MANTRA TO SHRI KRISHNA

One *mantra* very much recommended in certain Upanishads is the 8-syllabled "Om namo Narayanaya," which means "salutation to Narayana". Narayana is Vishnu, of whom Shri Krishna is considered the fullest avatara or incarnation. Vishnu is the middle member of the Trinity, the one Life and Light of the World. The Trinity itself is regarded as "not really so" but a "life-idol" to represent Parabrahman, transcending fact and thought. Shri Krishna, speaking in the *Bhagavad Gita*, gives us immense material for meditation on the subject of the one Self equally dwelling in all. After we have studied that and meditated upon it, namo Narayanaya will mean much to us and help to open the highest gates from thought into the Infinite.

A *mantra* which I received from Sir S. Subramania Iyer, who had it in turn from Shri T. Subba Row, who declared it to have been given to him as one of the "most powerful" of all *mantras*, is the 5-divisioned, 18-syllabled *mantra* to Shri Krishna, as follows:

KLĪM KRISHNĀYA, GOVINDĀYA, GOPĪ-JANA VALLABHĀYA, SWĀHĀ! [1]

Again and again the devotee repeats this *mantra*, and by it he attains to the path of Shri Krishna in this world. The following explanations are from the *Gopalatapani* and *Krishna* Upanishads.

"Once the Sages came to the great Brahma and asked: Who is the Supreme God? Whom does Death fear? Through the knowledge of what does all become known? What makes this world continue on its course?

"He replied: Shri Krishna verily is the Supreme God. Death is afraid of Govinda (Shri Krishna). By knowing the Lord of Gopi-jana (Shri Krishna) the whole is known. By Swaha the world goes on evolving.

"Then they questioned him again: Who is Krishna? Who is Govinda? Who is the Lord of Gopi-jana? What is Swaha?

"He replied: Krishna is he who destroys all wrong. Govinda is the knower of all things, who, on earth, is

---

[1] Pronounce î as ee; ri as between ri and ru, *i.e.*, vowel r; â as in " father "; a as in " India "; o as in " go ".

known through the great teaching. The Lord of Gopi-jana is he who guides all conditioned beings. Swaha is his power. He who meditates on these, repeats the *mantra*, and worships him, becomes immortal.

"Again they asked him: What is his form? What is his *mantra*? What is his worship?

"He replied: He who has the form of a protector of cows (the verses of the great teaching). The cloud-coloured youth (the colour of the fathomless deep). He who sits at the root of the tree (whose spreading branches are the creation and evolution of the age). He whose eyes are like the full-blown lotus (always resting in the pure lotus hearts of his devotees). He whose raiment is of the splendour of lightning (shining by its own light). He who is two-armed (the life and the form). He who is possessed of the sign of wisdom (with which the silent sages are initiated). He who wears a garland of flowers (the string of globes or planets). He who is seated on the centre of the golden lotus (at the heart of all). Who meditates upon him becomes free. His is the *mantra* of five parts. The first is Klim Krishnaya. Klim is the seed of attraction. The second is Govindaya. The third is Gopi-jana. The fourth is Vallabhaya. The fifth and last is Swaha. Klim—to Krishna—to the Giver of Knowledge—to the Lord of the Cowherds—Swaha.

"Om. Adoration to the Universal Form, the Source of all Protection, the Goal of Life, the Ruler of the Universe, and the Universe itself.

"Om. Adoration to the Embodiment of Wisdom, the Supreme Delight, Krishna, the Lord of Cowherds! To the Giver of Knowledge, adoration!"

MEDITATION ON SHRI KRISHNA

If you would practise this form of meditation, sit quietly in your usual place and let your thoughts and feelings simmer down until your mind dwells peacefully upon the thought of the great teacher.

Now imagine in the region of your own heart a rose-bud or a lotus bud. Let your mind look at it peacefully, as it droops upon its stem. Gradually, while you pronounce the word *Klim* with intent, longing for the presence of the divine, raise up the flower now blossoming, and see, sitting on that twelve-petalled throne, the divine form of Shri Krishna, the cloud-coloured youth with lotus eyes, wearing the garland of the worlds, sitting at the root of the tree of life, his raiment shining with the splendour of lightning. And as you bow before him, saying *Krishnaya*, offer your devotion to him. And as you say *Govindaya*, see him raise his hand with the sign of wisdom in blessing. And as you repeat *Gopi-jana Vallabhaya*, let the power of love irradiate you. And as you utter *Swaha*, expand your thought to include all life with you in your worship. Repeat several times the *mantra* of Shri Krishna, contemplating the divine form in the flower of your heart.

THE MEANING OF OM

Om is described as the indicator of Ishwara, a word translatable as God, Ruler, Vishnu, Shabda Brahman, Avalokiteshwara, etc. Om is not a name, not even a word with a conventional meaning, but an indicator.[1] And Ishwara is the supreme teacher in all of us, touching us not via mineral, plant, animal or human substance or form but, beyond these, *within*. I must explain. Each one of us is living in a large world of life. There is the mineral kingdom which is necessary to me. With it I live, not interfering with the functioning of its life. If, as a thinker using my combinative and constructive faculty, I move my stone paperweight from the writing pad to the book, the stone-consciousness still acts according to its own nature. I have not troubled it. We live with the vegetable and animal kingdoms also; without them there would be no bodily life for us. The same is true in our human relations, from the beginnings of the body derived from parents to the provision throughout life of nourishment to both body and mind. Life is all one, in which mineral, vegetable, animal and human are only phases, somewhat similar to the stages of childhood, youth, etc., in the body. It is only one step now to say that we are to the liberated men much as the lower kingdoms are to us, but their action, whatever it may be (not merely a glorified replica of our own constructiveness), is of a nature that does not interfere with our following our own nature. They do not work with us via mineral, vegetable or animal forms, but beyond our mind-operativeness in another mode of consciousness to which we will open ourselves in due course. What other meaning could there be to their realization that the same self is equally dwelling in all, or what the

[1] See *Practical Yoga, Ancient and Modern*, by Ernest Wood, (published by E. P. Dutton & Co., Inc., New York; also Rider & Co., London), for a translation and explanation of Patanjali's treatment of Ishwara as a subject of meditation, etc.

Hindu and Buddhist teachers meant by non-separate ness and "the universe grows I," or Christ by "one in the Father"?

And when it comes to Ishwara, he is ruler in his own life, not in ours—perhaps we should not use the word "his" with its limited implications. We must at last let go even that idol—like a child's doll—and enter into the meditation and contemplation for which the idol-thought was only a means of preliminary concentration, a process of "Thou art *That*," in which the realization of *That* sanctifies and sublimes the Thou.

I have not departed from consideration of the indicator Om. Om means "I am That" and "Thou art That," and in that mood must I begin my meditation with the *mantra* to Shri Krishna already explained.

That Om should be the indicator is provided for in its structure. It is a unique word, in that, being composed of 'a' plus 'u' plus 'm,' it begins with 'a,' the first articulation we can make in the back of the mouth, goes through the middle sound 'u,' and ends with the last sound we can make, 'm,' closing the mouth. 'A' followed rapidly by 'u' forms 'o,' and thus we have 'om,' which sounds like the English word "home" with the 'h' removed, and the 'm' a little prolonged. Thus Om goes from the beginning to the end of all articulate sounds, and includes all meanings and unity as well.

CHAPTER XII

OBSTACLES TO MEDITATION

THE THREE STEPS

IF you have resolved upon true success in life, that is, to achieve (1) that full living which is prescribed by the spiritual law of action with love and thought, along with (2) the never-closing of that gateway to the inner light that you have opened in your meditations, and if you know that not really you have resolved but something has resolved in you, and if you have said to yourself "I will," you will, if you look back, see that you have done three things. The first was to turn your face in the right direction. The second was to keep it there. The third was to make an effort to go forward—not to hurry, but just to drive forward and not stop for anything.

Constantly, for some time to come, you will need to revise these three steps: to see that you are going the right way, to keep from deviating, and to drive on. Put in as much force as you can when you are sure that you are going in the right direction, not before. If you drive forward when you are off the track, you will do damage to yourself and others, and make obstacles for yourself in the future; but if you keep straight there will be nothing to fear.

In order to keep straight remember the three points of the spiritual law. Remember that others also want the things which you seek. Let them have what they want. Never deprive another of that which you value for yourself, whether it be liberty or power, knowledge or learning, love or friendship. If you find yourself trying to gain power over others, seeking to surpass others in knowledge, or to attract the love or praise of others, you may know that you are in danger and must take especial care never to injure another by thought or word or act. Any breach of the law will be punished in some way, for there is no real greatness without goodness.

GIVE UP WISHING

I have said this before, but here it comes in again. Before you can pass on from meditation to contemplation you must be able to give up wishing and hoping entirely, at least during the period of practice. The mind can never be single while wishes occupy it. Every wish is also a seed from which may spring anger, untruthfulness, robbery, impurity, greed, carelessness, discontent, sloth, ignorance and resentment; and while one wish or hope remains within you, all these violations of the spiritual law are possible. Give up wishing and hoping; say: "I will," and have faith; stand out of your own light and let the spiritual law work its will and way.

If only you can maintain this attitude there will be no obstacles in your meditation, but if you have it not they will constantly come in and spoil your work. The stream of thought will try to flow aside into little gullies and channels left open by unsatisfied desires and indecisive thought. Every little unsatisfied desire, every unthought-out problem, will present a hungry mouth calling aside your attention; and inevitably in your meditation, when the train of thought meets with a difficulty, it will swing aside to attend to these calls.

To clear away these obstructions it is little use trying to repress and suppress them. A better plan is to give them their due, appoint them a time and think them out. A mind that cannot overcome such vacillation as leaves its problems perpetually unsettled cannot succeed in meditation. A man for this purpose must decide to arbitrate his problems, abide by his own decisions and refuse to think the same matter over and over again. The ability to do this grows with practice and with the habit of putting decisions into action. Fill up all the chinks of thought and bend the little side-rills round so that they discharge themselves into the main stream. Think out every problem and interruption in the light of its bearing and effect upon your main purpose. The development of a general philosophic mood which brings its experiences and faculties to a unity of understanding and purpose is essential for the successful pursuit of meditation. It is of great assistance also to know what type of man or woman you are, so that you will not try to cover too wide a field in your personal life. We are limited. And cannot be doctor, engineer, poet, artist, shop-keeper, lawyer and preacher all at once. Having chosen your type and sphere of activity keep to it unless you have good reason to change.

THE NEED OF A TEACHER

Among these unsatisfactions, one that stands out very prominently in the thoughts of many aspirants to higher consciousness is eagerness to find a teacher. It is the greatest encouragement to know that there must be those who have gone ahead of us and become part of that unseen spiritual life which is surely as intimate to our daily life as our material atmosphere and the earth under our feet. And all religions affirm that from that realm external inspired teachers appear to remind men of their spiritual nature, origin and destiny. But if we use this blessed knowledge wrongly, as so many do, and fall into the constant habit of craving for assistance, we shall find this to be one of the greatest obstacles to meditation and spiritual realization.

It is surely right that in the midst of our self-reliance we should always recognize the necessity of a teacher. But remember that you always have a teacher at your side, though that teacher is not necessarily a man at first or at any time. Perhaps you have found a book that for the time inspires you; let that be your teacher for the time being; do not crave for a teacher while neglecting the teacher at your hand. It has been credibly asserted that at an advanced stage in the aspirant's progress, when he has used to the full all the general knowledge that he finds in books or obtains from those who know the beginnings of the art, he will receive intuitive instruction from the world of life. The teachers are at hand every moment, and will speak with us when we prefer them to the things of confusion which at present we seek to grasp, to know and to fondle. They will not come before, because to do so would be an injury, not a benefit, to us.

In old India they had *gurukulas* or teachers' homes, to which pupils went for both secular and spiritual teaching. Those were the days when books were not generally available, but nowadays every one of us can have at hand the words of the greatest teachers of the world available in books. Still, commenting on the *Sanatsujatiya*,[1] a book belonging to ancient times, the famous teacher Shri Shankaracharya, wrote that the attainment of the pupil could be ascribed to four causes: one quarter to the maturity of understanding that comes by time, one quarter by associating with the teacher, one quarter by means of his own talent and effort, and one quarter by studying the subject-matter in consultation with his fellow-students.

When you have performed the three parts of using your own talents and studying with others for sufficient time to allow maturity of understanding, I should be much surprised to hear that you have not come into touch with a teacher to direct your final efforts, or at least advise when you are missing the way—the teacher who, it is said, when the pupil is ready is always there.

MEDITATE WITHIN YOURSELF

Yet another serious obstacle is the craving for some special method of meditation, and an eagerness to know whether to meditate in the heart, in the head, in the little finger, or in some other place. Do not trouble about these things at all, unless they are prescribed for you by a competent teacher; but meditate right down inside yourself. Go deep enough to forget your body for the time being; for remember the whole purpose of meditation is first to modify yourself, to alter your own shape

[1] *Op. cit.* Trans. K. T. Telang, Clarendon Press, Oxford, 1908.

of mind, and then to grow on the new axes that you have thus formed.

Be frank with yourself. Clearly define your purpose and settle upon the best means that lead thereto. Life is serious. You cannot afford to play with your destiny and palter with your principles. If you still seek above all things the satisfaction of worldly and personal ambitions and possessions acknowledge the fact to yourself and consistently pursue the objects to success. A mind divided against itself can spoil both outward and inward success. Success in meditation will not come until you disband the conflicting hosts of desires that perpetually carry on their civil wars within you, and thus come to be at peace with yourself. Then that peace within will put you at peace with all the world. You can be at peace with the world even when the world is not at peace with you.

CHAPTER XIII

CONTEMPLATION

THE TOP OF YOUR THOUGHT

THE old teachers of meditation held that there is a two-fold contemplation at the top end of our line of thought, one which gives intuition about the object, whereby the mind obtains its closest touch with that object, receiving its highest lesson, while the second leads to the beyond of the mind. Just as our body, having reached a certain point at which it serves the mind (which is the beyond of the body), need not grow any bigger or sprout any extra arms and legs, because the mind is now the life, so also the mind, having reached a certain point, ceases its own growth and lives on only to serve the beyond of the mind.

We can, if we like, go on developing the existing powers of the mind to the extent of genius, just as we can develop the body to become a great athlete, but that is so much bondage to personality according to the teachers and is not really to be wanted or admired. Having reached the point at which we are competent to serve and join with the beyond—the god within, beyond mind—we are foolish if we do not enter that service and give our allegiance and worship to that. Devotion to geniuses and worship of external superior beings partakes of the same error as the desire for personal greatness of body or mind. This is where hero-worship can go wrong.

INSPIRATION

In the beginning the fruits of contemplation are received into the mind as if from above, and they are most delicate to grasp and hard to hold. The following poem by Rands will help us to understand.

> Into the skies, one summer's day,
> I sent a little Thought away;
> Up to where, in the blue round
> The sun sat shining without sound.
>
> Then my Thought came back to me—
> Little Thought, what did you see
> In the regions whence you come?
> And when I spoke, my Thought was dumb.
>
> But she breathed of what was there,
> In the pure bright upper air;
> And, because my Thought so shone,
> I knew she had been shone upon.

The thought came back, bringing with it new shining, because it had been shone upon. It is something like sending up our thermometers and hygrometers and pressure guages into the upper atmosphere to bring back messages to us.

People who are given to much thought or meditation on any subject often go to the end of their thought, and their mind-hunger then prompts them to look into the apparent void beyond. This is the nature of the practice of contemplation, so that when you have completed your meditation on an object or subject, and cannot go further, you do not drop it with a sigh, but, poised in that condition, you look expectantly at it. Your conscious activity is preserved if you gaze quietly at your highest thought. Then comes a moment of self-forgetfulness which is really the dropping of your limited viewpoint, and you receive an intuition, insight or illumination. Beauty, love, power, peace, understanding—something within these groups then comes to you.

Once I was walking with a friend along a street of houses, some with gardens containing trees. At one place we heard a bird, beautifully singing. My friend said: "It must be a bird in a cage. We could not expect a free bird like that in a place like this." And then I thought, "The bird is here in a cage. It is like an inspiration. When it comes we must capture it and put it in a cage of words." And then, "I must go often to that cage and listen to the captive bird. Some day I shall become more attuned to it, and not so much a stranger. Then my bird can go free, and it will come when I call, and perhaps I may visit it in its own garden before long." Our inspirations are to be cherished and lived with until we are fully attuned to them.

There is no shortage of testimony to these intuitions. I will content myself with one example, from the musical composer, Wagner. Writing to Frau Wesendonck, he said: "The Tristan drama is and remains a marvel to me. I am more and more unable to understand how I could produce such a thing." All such high experiences lead to deep thoughts. Wagner further wrote: "I often turn with longing to the land of Nirvana. . . It is the bliss of quitting life. . . of last redemption in the wondrous realm from which we wander farthest when we strive to enter it with fiercest force. Shall we call it Death? Or is it not night's wonder world?" The greatest art is artless, and comes as a surprise to the artist. This is a principle that applies to all the varieties of our spiritual hunger.

We need not question as to whether our inspiration comes from a deeper working of our own mind, a direct perception of some truth, or is "picked out of the ether" where the thoughts of all high minds somehow dwell. Enough that it is beyond all personality and personal interests and ownership, and cannot be known by any trade-mark or label. It is one of the most inspiring things to know that only steps of truth can carry us to a goal of truth, only steps of love to the height of love, and only steps of private courage to freedom. We have to be true to ourselves before anything in the world—whether thing or person—can be true to us.

Again, we must not ask for a particular inspiration. It is a condition of inspiration that we must take what it brings. Hoping and wishing for this or that message or instruction, or presuming what is likely to come, can only shut the door of truth.

Intellectual Contemplation

There are certain definite ways in which we can practise contemplation. In all cases one should go through the three stages in order to reach the top of one's thought:

(1) the attention must be centred on the object; (2) thought must be active with reference to that object alone; (3) the mind must come to an end of its remembering, collating, comparing, reasoning and meditating, but still remain attentively poised upon the object.

It will be seen that throughout the three stages the mood of concentration continues so that the activity of mind is maintained within the chosen sphere of attention. The process of contemplation will really commence when thought ceases to expand or amplify the subject-matter of the object, and yet the mind remains poised. Then the conscious activity begins to run, as it were, at right angles to the usual thought-activity which endeavours to understand and think in reference to other things of its own nature or "plane". When the attention is no longer divided into parts by the mental activities, the mind will be moving as a whole, and will seem quite still, just as a spinning top may appear to stand still when it is in most rapid motion.

Suppose, for example, you take an idea such as that of justice; you might first consider some form of justice, the manifestation of justice in an act, in such a manner that the whole of your mind is occupied with that; then you might turn to the thought of the psychological effects of justice on the doer and the receiver, and allow this to occupy the entire mind; and then pass from that to an endeavour to comprehend abstract justice, and thus continue the mental effort until you can carry your thought no further, but find it in, as it were, an open space, and unable to grasp anything clearly. When you then, by an effort of will, hold your thought at a level beyond that at which its normal activities go on, it is obvious that then you can no longer be thinking about the object, but only contemplating it.

If you are able to do so, it will be better to avoid starting this process with the thought of yourself and the object as two different things in relation to each other, for then you will not easily escape this idea of its relation to yourself, and thus will not be able to obtain the idea untinctured with feeling. But if you can reach such a point of self-detachment as to start your contemplation from the inside of the thing itself, and still keep up your mental enthusiasm and energy all along the line of thought, from the name to the form of the object, from that to its psychological aspect (to its feeling or thought, if it is a sentient object, or to the feeling and thought which it awakens in a sentient mind, if it is a mere object or a quality) from that to its abstract nature (to its nature in simultaneous relation to all conceivable manifestations of itself) in which both word and form have disappeared—and you are able to hold the mind there, trying to pierce the indefiniteness that surrounds this state (and yet using no words or forms for that purpose), just as you might try to penetrate a mist with physical vision, then, holding yourself there, looking forward and never thinking of turning back, poised, as it were, like a bird on the wing, you will accomplish contemplation.

Let us take some definite examples in order to make the method more comprehensible. If I fix my attention on this sheet of paper, I may consider what sort, size, shape, colour, texture, thickness, variety, of paper it is, what relation it bears to other sheets of paper in the book, where and how it was made, and many other things in connection with it. Suppose, however, I wish to contemplate it, then I will start with my attention on the paper and, after observing it, carefully proceed to think of its more subtle nature, of its composition, of the subtle elements that make it up, and what it would be like to a vision which had to do with such subtle realities. Going beyond that, I might try to conceive what is the nature of those invisible particles composing it, and make an effort to apply to them a kind of mental perception, not mere words and definitions. Such a course would end in the process of contemplation.

If, however, an object possessing consciousness is selected, more stages will be available. Suppose, for example, we take a dog. I concentrate my attention on the dog, not thinking of that dog in relation to myself as regards action or emotion or position or relatively of any kind. I pass from that to an effort to understand the inner nature of the object, the feelings and thoughts that may occupy it, and endeavour to realize its state of consciousness. It is difficult to go further with an animal.

If one ventures to fix one's attention upon a superior being, one would pass from the physical appearance to meditate upon the state of feeling and emotion and thought, and so try to rise inwards to grasp the state of consciousness which he enjoys. In any of these cases, when I have carried my thought inwards until it can go no further and I cannot grasp clearly what is before it, though I know that there is something there, and hold to that position without going back or turning aside, I am in a state of contemplation with reference to the inner nature of that object. This is a process which must generally be practised many times, whenever opportunity offers, before success will come.

If I look at a statue in a museum, I find that the artist and the curators have already done some concentration for me. They have put that object there, away from the madding crowd of similar things, and away from the multifarious business of the outside day. In the museum I am in the mood for looking. My mind becomes poised on the statue, and for me some part or curved line of it comes to stand out. I look closer or more attentively at this, with a kind of listening reaching look. I have caught some beauty; but heaven preserve me from saying that to myself, for if I do the inner gate is closed. Rather let the beauty catch me, and carry me, in unconsciousness of my old self, into . . . well, I just cannot say what; it has no thisness to answer to any sort of what.

Such contemplation sometimes occurs spontaneously in ordinary life, when the mind is "enraptured" or "entranced" by contemplation of a beautiful thing or a flood of understanding. Its character is always the same— we "forget ourselves" yet are most fully alive. When we return to the state of "I am this"—"this" being the idea-personality that we normally regard as self, and begin to say "I see" or "I know" with reference to contemplation-experience, the clouds gather again before the face of the true sun. Does it not hurt us when we are contemplating something beautiful in Nature or art, and somebody starts talking about it: "See, is it not beautiful, wonderful, grand?" Must we come back from consorting with beauty itself to grub among ideas? Only the building of a new "I" with materials of contemplative experience will bring to us the possibility of living in the "beyond" of the mind.

It will be seen that in this contemplation there is nothing in the nature of sleep or mental inactivity, but an intense search; you make an effort to see in the indefiniteness something definite, and refuse for the time being to descend to the ordinary lower regions of conscious activity in which your sight is normally clear and precise.

An Explanation

An esteemed friend has asked me: "Is it not correct to do that sort of Meditation in which one stills one's own thinking, and remains in a state of active expectancy of an intuition?" This arose apropos of a statement of mine that Patanjali had taught Meditation as a continued mental effort to understand some subject, not as a voluntary stoppage of mentality.

The answer is: "Yes, it is correct, though not for everybody nor with regard to all subjects, but only for one who has previously done the thinking." It is a case of yearning being followed by triumph, which is the secret of all evolution, in which something new comes in as it were from above. The state of active expectancy belongs to Contemplation. The Intuition received in that state would mean nothing to a mind not having the correct prior content. When the Intuition comes it illumines the field of existing knowledge. The moment of rapture or illumination comes when the consciousness ceases to be interested in itself as the doer of the meditation and thus the effort to understand or know can come to its fulfilment without the limitation of the bias

due to personal interest in it.   It is then a case of purity
of intent to know or understand.   There is then a passage from rajasic or ambitious thinking to sattwic or
peaceful thinking.   There is an intimacy of the knowing.

An example of this is the understanding of a piece of
music as music.   If we have not heard *well* the successive notes of the piece of music we cannot "get" the
music, which involves the grasping of a unity, which is
the essence of understanding.   Unity is the key to understanding, always; it is the complete seeing or knowing.
So one would not recommend the method of expectancy
except to a student or thinker who has conscientiously
tried to understand the matter in which he is to receive
an intuition.

In experiments in telepathy the receptor is told not to
think about anything, yet not to be passive, but to be in
a condition of active expectancy, like that of a person
looking through a window to see what may pass by.
This person will understand what he sees only in terms
of prior knowledge.   But one who has fully thought
can receive something new, because each faculty is the
seed-bed of the next to come.   Thought comes up to
resolve our emotional problems; love comes in to resolve
our mental impasses; the intuition of Destiny comes in
to resolve our problems of love.   These come in a little
at first, but every time as something new, and later in
full fountain—whereupon the consciousness steps up
into its new function, which is no longer an intuition
but is now a power.   Now, in the course of fulfilling
that function, it becomes the receptor of flashes (sparks)
of the next new faculty for which it has become the seed-
bed.   When one power is being used (not otherwise),

the next is being prepared behind the scenes. In the course of growth the following is the natural successor. First comes action, then emotion, then thought, then love, then the faith-knowledge, corresponding to the five principles of man (and all the others), physical, emotional, mental, moral (which is also ethical), and spiritual.

DEVOTIONAL CONTEMPLATION

One who has an intense affection for an object of worship can follow the same method, but in his case the activity will be mainly one of feeling. The devotee will first picture in imagination the particular form which he regards as ideal. He will dwell upon that, allowing his feelings to flow out in affection, admiration and reverence. He will picture himself as in the company of that ideal or perfect being, associated with him in the incidents of his life. Then, when his feelings are at their height, he will make an effort to pass from the outer form to realize the feelings and thoughts which animated that form. He will begin to realize, with ardent devotion, the nature of the divine nature as something more than a bigger or finer ordinary nature.

A simple worshipper at first regards God, manifested in a particular form, as the proprietor of all things, and desires to perform all the acts of his life in order to please. Next he begins to see that the finer qualities, which he first discovered in the divine form, are to be seen in some measure in other forms also, and he then begins to realize that there is something of divine nature in all things—that God pervades where he possesses. Thus expanding his devotion the worshipper begins to perceive God in all forms and to feel for them an ardent affection, insomuch as they manifest him.

Slowly another dawn breaks upon the devotee, and now, instead of feeling that there is something of God in all forms he will realize that all exists in God, that each represents and reproduces him, though not in his fullness, yet just so much of it as there is, is God, and if anything seems to be evil or ugly that is because he feels there a little absence of something else of what he knows to be divine. In these lesser things it is as though the devotee, though looking only at the feet of his God, yet loves the whole of him. He is learning the absolute presence of the divine.

One may put the same thought in terms of nirvana and maya. The attainment of nirvana implies a dissolution of maya, which has the two factors of covering up part of the reality and building on the remains. Maya is like a reticulated veil over the face of reality. However many be the veils it is always the same face, the same reality, that is seen, though darkly, incompletely, imperfectly. When the maya of mind is removed, the consciousness that is strong enough to bear the light of reality will be with it face to face, beyond sensation, memory, imagination and reasoning. Maya is disharmony through absence, neglect, ignoring. Harmony always incarnates unity. Unity is the power of the unmanifest working in the manifest. That is why contemplation should be preceded by meditation. Harmony reached in the mind is peace of mind, and in that harmony the unity is revealed, unveiled.

In the course of his practice there will be times when the devotee will lose grasp, as he goes onward, of the things which have been in special and superior moments clear to him. He will find himself in a state of emotional flatness. But memory will tell him that this is only temporary and encourage him not to despond, but continue trying to penetrate what may sometimes seem to be a grey and empty sky.

CONTEMPLATION AND WORSHIP

Contemplation is always to be seen to some extent in true worship. Worship is a faculty different from thought, different even from love; it is the little self finding itself within the greater self, as though the sun reflected in a pool of water should look up at the sun in heaven and feel a sudden liberation into that great life. It has not lost itself; it has gained itself. This is the experience of a man suddenly confronted with a realization of that which is utterly greater than he had thought. Thus he occasionally forgets that which he used to call himself, and this more and more frequently, so that it becomes only a sub-conscious element, as it were, in the new life.

It is the opening up of a new faculty. With the physical body we contact the material things of the world; with our lower emotions we rejoice in their energy; with our mentality we deal with the "material laws" that govern all those things; with our higher emotions we become sensitive to the life in our neighbour and devoted to a joint welfare and happiness; but with this faculty of worship we break through the duality of devotion into the unity of self and God. No longer is it "Thy will be done," but the actuality of what is a paradox to the lower mind: "Thy will and mine are one." In certain advanced circles "O Thou" is the greatest heresy.

Emerson spoke of this faculty as the flowering and completion of human culture. On the tree of life it is not always the biggest branch that is the highest. At the animal stage of evolution we see that the physical and emotional powers have been developed, and there is also a growth of mind. At the ordinary human level that growth of mind has become dominant, and the man uses his judgment to select his desires, to decide which feelings he will keep in his mind and which he will set aside, but in him there is yet only a tiny appearance of the higher human emotion, the ethical instinct that can make him consider others as himself. In the man of saintly type that ethical instinct has grown till it overshadows the mentality and in him the mind is occupied only in planning for the service of that great human heart. But even he has still to develop to its full proportions another faculty—this realization of the divine Self, the faculty of worship.

CONTEMPLATION OF THE SELF

Another form of contemplation, in great favour in the school of Shri Shankaracharya, is the contemplation of one's own true nature. Look at the body and consider its various parts. Gaze at the hand; look at it intently as mere dissociated form, until you realize that "such a queer thing cannot be I". Apply the same thought to any part of the body. Look in a mirror at your own eyes and realize that they, also, cannot be

11

yourself. Subject and object can never be the same, and I am the subject, the perceiver, not the form, the perceived.

What then are you? The invisible mind which uses this aggregate called the body? Inspect the mind as you have examined the body. You have discovered that you are not fingers and thumbs and eyes. Are you anger, fear, trust, doubt, kindness, reverence, pride, or any other of the various modes of action of the mind? Are you to be found in its modes of receiving knowledge? Are you reason, or perception, or the faculty of discrimination? Surely not. These are the elements which aggregate to compose the mind, and thus this mind cannot be myself. The mind is only an aggregate, a collection of objective things, an external thing, and not myself. I look down upon it and know that it is not myself. When I walk across the room I can ask myself the question: "Am I walking?" and answer, "No, I am not walking; I am watching the body walk." Similarly, I am watching the mind think.

Whence, then, does the conception of individuality arise? Am I this personality, this John Smith or Lord Whiptop? Certainly not; this is a mere collection of associations which I am temporarily using, having gathered them round myself and shut myself in with them by a long series of imperfect imaginings. No other person can speak of me, can praise or blame me; they know only this outer thing. If I in the past have fallen in love with this body and mind, become infatuated with it, as Narcissus with his reflection in the pool, still there is no need that I should continue the error. What then is the I, when you have thus struck away these temporary external coverings? That question can be answered only by each one for himself when he realizes his own inner nature, having cast away layer after layer of the outer crust, having broken away the shell to find the kernel within. Then arises the question, "Is that an endless series?" The answer is, "No; for series is a mental conception. You must not try to carry your series-conception into the beyond of the mind. It is more like the chicken in the egg-shell. One peck more—that last peck!—and the chick goes through into its beyond."

It would be a mistake to suppose that, as that process of inner search for yourself goes on, your own nature is discovered to be more indefinite. Such an idea arises from the erroneous supposition that only the outer body is warm and full of the wine of life, while the inner is chill and empty. Some philosophers have ventured to say that they cannot detect themselves apart from some bodily feeling, but that is only another way of saying that one cannot remain awake in the body without some sensibility of the body, that one cannot think of the body without feeling it in some way, which is no doubt true. But it is possible to lose sight for a time of the existence of the body and find oneself something beyond it.

What are the results of denying, in this contemplation, our identity with the outer bodies and the mind? What is the effect of this realization that the mind with all its contents is a thing that we use, not that we are? Does it mean that the inner man is left more and more attribute-less—changeless, powerless, loveless, ignorant? It does not. In the process you are not divesting yourself of attributes but of limitations. The mind is swifter and freer than the body, and beyond the mind is the spirit, which is freer and swifter still. Love is more possible in the quietude of the heart than in any outer expression, but in the spirit beyond the mind it is divinely certain. Reason and judgment ever correct the halting evidence of the senses, and the vision of the spirit will discern the truth without organs and without mind.

CHAPTER XIV

CONCLUSION

IF you have said: "I will," then choose what you will have, and the nearer your choice is to the spiritual heart of things the sooner you will succeed. Give rein to your fancy and picture to yourself the liberty, and the might, and the love, and the knowledge that will be yours. Your chariot shall be the lightning flash, and your raiment the splendour of the sun, and your voice shall be the thunder of the spheres. The divinest knowledge shall be your food, and the ethereal blue your home. Yours shall be the strength of mountains, the power of the tempest, the force of the ocean, the beauty of the sunrise, the triumph of the noonday sun, the liberty of the wind, the gentleness of the flowers, the peace of the evening twilight, the purity of eternal snow.

Do you say that this is extravagant? It is not so. It is true that you may not achieve this success in one brief life time. But believe in your own immortality, then realize that the future is full of splendour without limit, of achievement beyond, and beyond, and beyond again, the most avaricious dreams of imagination, yet that the achievement is a matter for your choosing now. Death is but a trifling episode in our agelong life. Through its portal we will go as one rises from a bed of sickness to go out into the sunshine. If we set our hearts upon the superhuman things, then we shall achieve. If we fix our ambitions in human life, these, no doubt, we shall attain. Rather, believe in your own immortality; give wings to your imagination; say: "This is within my reach, I WILL ACHIEVE"—and success will come sooner than you expect. Do you dread time? If so, you have not willed but only wished, for if you had willed you would know that the result is certain, and what is sure is as good as though it were already here. Fix your thought upon your aim; it will come, and its time is as good as now, and, in the light of that certainty, what may happen to us between now and then can matter not at all, and of no moment can be the road we take to that stupendous goal.

OTHER QUEST BOOK TITLES

For a complete descriptive list of all Quest Books write to:

QUEST BOOKS

P.O. Box 270, Wheaton, Illinois, 60187